Praise for *This Fleeting World*

I first became an avid student of David Christian by watching his course, Big History, *on DVD, so I am very happy to see his enlightening presentation of the world's history captured in these essays. I hope it will introduce a wider audience to this gifted scientist and teacher.*

Bill Gates, founder of Microsoft

No one except David Christian could do it. He has a unique talent for mastering data, processing it efficiently, and writing it up lucidly. He can simplify without dumbing down and can be provocative without sliding into outrage. Readers can rely on him for a sensitive, well-informed, well-judged, reflective, and miraculously concise overview.

Felipe Fernández-Armesto, professor of modern history, University of Notre Dame

David Christian has developed fascinating new perspectives on the global past by systematically considering human history in the context of the natural environment. This Fleeting World *offers a succinct articulation of his views, which hold fresh ideas for professional historians and the general public alike.*

Jerry H. Bentley, editor, *Journal of World History*

"Big history" is best when it's small [and David] Christian's little book is the narrative that best meets the growing contemporary demand for a short "big history." . . . The best thing of all about this book, I think, is that it does not "cover" anything. Instead, This Fleeting World *deploys sparkling prose to entice the student to enlist in her or his education, to take on the project of finding his or her place in the world that is, and has been for 250,000 years, so increasingly full.*

William Everdell in *World History Connected*

(continued)

David Christian is the Copernicus of "big history." His approach is so capacious, conceptually rigorous, and challenging as to force the reconsideration of all histories written on a lesser scale.

Terry Burke, University of California, Santa Cruz

This Fleeting World *provides world history teachers and students the "big picture" that world history demands: big enough to incorporate historical content beyond just the last few thousand years; yet simple enough to be easily understood by average readers. Christian's analysis is a pleasure to read because it presents history in an approachable way without denying its subtle complexity and ambiguity.*

Bill Strickland, College Board Consultant for
AP World History

Specifically designed to aid teachers in lesson design, the book can easily be read in one sitting and should prove to be a valuable classroom resource.

VOYA (Voice of Youth Advocates)

Like great art, this book eliminates all that is unnecessary and strips history down to its most essential components, revealing a hitherto unseen commonality of experience in the unfolding of the human drama. David Christian's text offers an expansive conceptual framework that provides meaning and unity to the otherwise disconnected fragments of human history. This Fleeting World *is a powerful response to the postmodernist conception of history as disconnected and fragmented; it reveals a sense of purpose and meaning behind the seemingly random and chaotic nature of the human historical experience.*

Craig Benjamin, Grand Valley State University

This Fleeting World

⚔ A Short History of Humanity ⚓

This Fleeting World

❧ A Short History of Humanity ❧

David Christian

BERKSHIRE PUBLISHING GROUP

Great Barrington, Massachusetts

Published by:
Berkshire Publishing Group LLC
122 Castle Street
Great Barrington, Massachusetts 01230
www.berkshirepublishing.com

Project Coordinator: Rachel Christensen
Editor: Marcy Ross
Copy Editors: Francesca Forrest and Mike Nichols
Designers: Gabriel Every and Anna Myers
Compositor: Brad Walrod/High Text Graphics, Inc.
Proofreader: Mary Bagg
Indexer: Peggy Holloway
Printer: Thomson-Shore, Inc.

Printed in the United States of America

Library of Congress Cataloging-in-Publication Data
Christian, David, 1946–
    This fleeting world : a short history of humanity/ David Christian.—
1st ed.
        p. cm.
    Includes bibliographical references and index.
    ISBN 978-1-933782-04-1
    1. World history.   2. Civilization—History.   I. Title.
    D20.C498 2005
    909—dc22   2004025324

Thus shall ye think of all this fleeting world:
A star at dawn, a bubble in a stream,
A flash of lightning in a summer cloud,
A flickering lamp, a phantom, and a dream.
• THE DIAMOND SUTRA

Contents

Introduction

This Fleeting World was written in the belief that we urgently need to understand the history of all human beings. Nations and peoples are now so interconnected, and share so many problems, that we must learn not just what divides us but also what unites all humans within a single global community. A sense of shared humanity, of "global citizenship," will become more and more important in coming decades if we are to avoid major global crises, whether caused by warfare or ecological collapse (or both). To understand what unites us as humans, we need to understand that humans have a "big history" of our own, one that transcends the histories of particular regions, nations, ethnic groups, and even worlds. As H. G. Wells wrote in *The Outline of History* just after World War I, "there can be no common peace and prosperity without common historical ideas. Without such ideas to hold them together in harmonious co-operation, with nothing but narrow, selfish, and conflicting nationalistic traditions, races and peoples are bound to drift towards conflict and destruction."

As Henry Ford is supposed to have said, possibly around the time Wells wrote those words, history often seems to consist of just "one damn fact after another." (We wonder if Ford ever read *The Outline of History*, and if so what he thought of it.) That sort of history doesn't make much sense. So students often wonder why they're learning it, and teachers sometimes wonder why they're teaching it. History is worth learning and teaching if it can tell you something interesting, or inspiring, or worth learning, about the world you live in, the universe that surrounds you, and how everything came to be as it is. If the details are to make sense, you have to be able to see them as part of a larger story, the story of particular peoples or nations or groups or even worlds.

But which stories and which groups? Historians tell stories at many different scales. Some write about particular communities or historical events, such as World War I, or the rise of the Aztec empire. Some write at larger scales, covering entire eras or regions, such as the history of ancient

Rome or the United States. These are reasonably familiar stories, and it's relatively easy to write down the "story" of the United States or even of "Western civilization." Then there is a third scale, widely known today as "world history." World historians explore connections between different parts of the world and different eras so that you can better understand how the details are linked into a larger story. Of course, that is a huge—and daunting—task, and the "story" of world history contains many more "facts" than do the stories of particular nations or states. That's why telling this story is much more difficult. *This Fleeting World* was designed specifically to help students tackling world history.

The task becomes even more daunting when we broaden things even further to the burgeoning field known as "big history." Big history courses integrate human history and the planet's history into the narrative of the universe's creation. A typical big history course surveys the past on multiple scales. It begins by describing the origins of our universe 13.8 billion years ago in what cosmologists call "the Big Bang," described in the pages ahead. Then it describes the emergence of more complex entities as the simple early universe (made up of little more than hydrogen and helium atoms and lots of energy) began to generate increasingly complex phenomena. Many students find that big history courses validate the large questions about life, the Earth, and the universe that they desperately want to explore and that most university courses seem to ignore. But for precisely this reason, they want to discuss where the story is going: they want to talk about the future. And this of course brings history into the realm of environmental studies, which is full of questions with an urgent need for answers. What is the "Anthropocene epoch"? Will we run out of cheap energy or will new technologies allow sustained (and sustainable) growth? There are no firm answers to such questions, but having a grasp on world history and the even bigger "big history" that surrounds our world goes a long way toward gaining a grasp on these sorts of issues.

Some people doubt that there is even a coherent story out there to be told, even if we bring things back to the level of our own Earth's history. But there surely is, and in an era of globalization its importance is becoming more and more apparent. *This Fleeting World* tries to help readers grasp the shape of world and universal history by offering a concise history of humanity. It does so in order to help readers navigate through the blizzard of facts they will find in larger texts on world history. To navigate in unfamiliar terrain you need a map and a compass. So *This Fleeting World* offers a sort of navigational kit. It tries to do what a world map does when you study geography: it provides a large outline so you can keep a sense of the larger landscape as you study the details. Or perhaps you can think of it as a journey by plane over country you have already crossed on foot. From the plane you will not see many details, but you will get a clearer sense of the landscape. Individual objects may be blurred, but you will see the relationships between them more easily.

No survey this brief can do more than sketch some of the main lines of development of our remarkable species, and it is probable that different historians would have drawn the lines in different ways. Nevertheless, as the fields of world (and big) history have evolved during the last fifty years or so, some consensus has emerged on the crucial turning points in human history. The three main chapters of *This Fleeting World* are intended to distill something of that consensus. Brevity has its drawbacks, of course, but it also has its advantages. Above all, it should be possible to read this survey in one or two sittings, a short enough period to remember the beginning of the story as you reach the end!

Using *This Fleeting World*

This Fleeting World began as a series of overview essays written for the first edition of the *Berkshire Encyclopedia of World History*. World history teachers found the essays of such value in curriculum development, classroom preparation, and student review that we decided to publish them as a book. Following the main text, which takes the reader from the origins of the universe all the way through the modern day, we have included three appendices of material that will be helpful to students and teachers both.

Bob Bain and Lauren McArthur Harris—former world history teachers who now study teacher training methods—provide a study guide to give teachers comprehensive guidance on using *This Fleeting World* as a teaching tool. That study guide appears in this fifth printing as Appendix A. Appendix B discusses the complex issue of periodization: the decisions we make as we divide the past into manageable chunks. Appendix C includes references for further reading, including websites such as that of the Big History Project.

Despite its limitations, we hope teachers and students will find in *This Fleeting World* a helpful, if crude, sketch map of world history, perhaps a bit like the maps used by sixteenth-century world navigators. In their time, those maps worked surprisingly well, though they were eventually superseded, as this will be, by maps that were much more precise and vastly more sophisticated.

We hope you enjoy reading *This Fleeting World*, and we hope it will give you some sense of the vast, complex, sometimes tragic, but often inspiring history of the huge nation called "humanity," of which all of us are members.

Prequel: Before the Beginning

Beyond the history of humanity there is an even larger scale, embracing the history of the Earth and even the whole universe. This "prequel" sets the scene for the history of humanity by describing the past at this even larger scale: the field of "big history." Just as we need world history to help us understand the significance of particular local histories, so, too, we need an even larger map to help us see the place of human history in the history of the Earth and the universe. We need big history if we are to think beyond the bounds of our own human history.

Before the middle of the twentieth century, most astronomers thought that the universe didn't have a history. It had always existed. But there were reasons to doubt that theory. In the 1920s an American astronomer, Edwin Hubble, found evidence that the most remote galaxies were all flying away from us. That evidence suggested the bizarre idea that perhaps the universe was expanding. But if it was expanding, then in the past it must have been much smaller. And at some point in the very distant past it must have all been crushed into a tiny space perhaps smaller than an atom.

In the middle of the twentieth century, enough evidence accumulated to convince most astronomers that this was exactly what had happened. It turned out that humans were not the only creatures with a history. The planet had a history, and so did the universe as a whole. Since the middle of the twentieth century, we have been able to tell that history and to see human history as part of a much larger, scientific, "creation story." This "prequel" to human history offers a summary of that larger story as we understand it early in the twenty-first century. (Almost every human society has had a set of stories that explain the origins of the cosmos; these creation stories—never "myths" to those who believe them—attempt to give meaning to all of existence and often reflect the cultures from which they derive.)

The universe appeared about 13.8 billion (13,800,000,000) years ago in what cosmologists call, whimsically, "the Big Bang." This is the first of all historical dates. We don't know what there was before the Big Bang.

1

We don't know if there was time or space or even emptiness. We simply run out of information and theories; this is where creation stories come in. But from the moment the universe appeared we can tell a story that fits in with the fundamental ideas of modern science and is based on a huge—and increasing—amount of evidence.

When the universe appeared, it was tiny, probably smaller than an atom. Within it was all the matter/energy from which our universe would be made. But the universe was so hot (countless billions of degrees hot!) that matter, energy, particles, space, and time all seemed to be jumbled together. Bursting with energy, the universe expanded explosively, perhaps faster than the speed of light. As it expanded, it cooled. And, just as steam eventually condenses into water, so the universe, too, passed through a series of "phase changes" as it cooled. Within the first second of its existence, distinct forces appeared, including gravity (which tends to pull everything together) and electromagnetism (which draws opposite charges together but drives similar charges apart). Quarks, the basic constituents of matter, also appeared. But at first the universe was so violent that most particles annihilated themselves as soon as they appeared, turning into pure energy as they did so.

By the end of the first second, the rate of expansion had slowed. The universe already contained things we can recognize today, including

Thought Experiment

People try to understand their place in the universe and don't always agree. Consider the view of author Mark Twain (1835–1910), who wrote that humans would always see themselves as the center of the Universe—or at least the whole of history. In his 1903 essay, "Was the World Made for Man?" he wrote, "If the Eiffel Tower were now representing the world's age, the skin of paint on the pinnacle-knob at its summit would represent man's share of that age, and anybody would perceive that that skin was what the tower was built for. I reckon they would." Now imagine responding to Mark Twain's essay. Do we humans always have to see ourselves as the center of the universe? Or do you think you could suggest another perspective? Does it matter how we see our place in the universe?

protons and electrons (the basic components of every atom of matter) and at least four basic forms of energy. It was still hotter than the center of the sun and consisted of a "plasma," a chaotic mixture of energy and charged particles. After about 380,000 years it underwent another "phase change." It cooled enough for positively charged protons to capture negatively charged electrons, thereby forming the first atoms. These were electrically neutral, so quite suddenly matter ceased to interact with electromagnetic radiation. The energy released at this point in the universe's history can still be detected today in the so-called cosmic background radiation. The "CBR" shows up as static on old television sets, and its existence is one of the most powerful proofs that this story is true.

At this stage matter took extremely simple forms. Most matter consisted of free-floating hydrogen and helium atoms. Hydrogen atoms consist of just one proton and one electron, whereas helium atoms consist of two protons and two electrons. For millions of years the early universe consisted of little more than huge clouds of hydrogen and helium atoms. With no stars the universe was lit only by a faint glow from the huge amounts of energy pouring through it.

Then, in one of the most miraculous twists in this modern creation story, things began to get more complex. The first complex things to appear were stars. The architect of the first stars was gravity. Isaac Newton showed in the seventeenth century that every piece of matter exerts a sort of pull on every other piece of matter. That's why we stay attached to the Earth. Albert Einstein showed in the early twentieth century that matter and energy are really just different forms of the same underlying essence, which is why energy also exerts a gravitational pull. So, every bit of energy and matter in the early universe was exerting a gentle pull on every other bit. Gradually, gravity pulled together the huge clouds of hydrogen and helium atoms that drifted through the early universe. Billions of these clouds appeared, each contracting under the force of gravity. As they contracted, they began to heat up. The atoms inside each cloud began to move faster and faster, colliding with each other more and more violently. Eventually, when the center of each cloud reached about $10°$ C, hydrogen atoms began to fuse together, and as they did so, part of each atom was transformed into pure energy. This fusion is exactly what happens inside a hydrogen bomb. The energy now being released by these huge "hydrogen bombs" in the center of each cloud resisted the force of gravity, and energy began to pour out into the cold, empty space between the clouds. The first stars had been born, about 200 million years after the universe was created. Most, like our own Sun, would keep burning for many billions of years.

Under the gentle tug of gravity, stars collected into "galaxies," with billions of individual stars, like our own galaxy, the "Milky Way." Galaxies, in turn, collected into "clusters" of galaxies. But at the very largest scales, the tug of gravity was too weak to counteract the expansion of the universe, so, although clusters of galaxies are held together by gravity, the gap between clusters tends to widen as the universe expands.

Stars began to generate a new form of complexity by creating new elements. The largest stars generated the most pressure, so they tended to be hottest. At their heart, fusion reactions occurred more rapidly until, some millions of years after they were created, they ran out of hydrogen. At this point their centers collapsed, generating even higher temperatures, until helium atoms began to fuse to form more complicated elements, such as carbon. In a series of violent collapses like this, new elements were created up to iron, which has twenty-six protons in its nucleus. Creating elements with more protons requires temperatures that no star, however big, can generate. When a large star collapses, however, it dies in a colossal explosion known as a "supernova." That's where the remaining elements can be made, all the way up to uranium, which has ninety-two protons in its nucleus. So, the chemicals from which we are made were manufactured in the death throes of large stars. Supernovae made chemistry possible. Without them, we would not exist, nor would the Earth.

The first supernovae probably blew up within a billion years of the Big Bang. Ever since, supernovae have been seeding the space between stars with more complex chemicals so that, although hydrogen and helium remain by far the most common elements in the universe, there has built up a significant residue of other elements as well. These could combine in complex ways to form the chemicals from which new—and more complex—things could be made, including ourselves.

Planets were the first objects made from these more complex materials. In galaxies such as the Milky Way, interstellar space was seeded with all these new chemical elements. So, when new stars were created, they formed not from clouds of just hydrogen and helium, but from clouds that also contained carbon, oxygen, nitrogen, gold, silver, uranium, in fact, all the elements of the "periodic table." Our Sun was formed about 4.5 billion years ago from just such a cloud of matter. This "solar nebula" (as it is called) contracted under the pull of gravity until hydrogen atoms began to fuse at the center to form the star we call "the Sun." Most of the solar nebula was gobbled up by the Sun, but tiny amounts of matter continued to orbit the young Sun farther out. In each orbit atoms collided, stuck together, and slowly formed into larger objects, a bit like snowballs. (In fact, some comets are really little more than huge snowballs, remnants of this stage of our planet's history.) These collided and stuck together to form larger objects such as meteorites or asteroids, which we call "planetesimals." Gradually, in each orbit, all the bits and pieces collided and stuck together to form a series of planets in a process known as "accretion." The heat of the sun drove the gassier elements away from the center, which is why the inner planets (Mercury, Venus, Earth, Mars) are rockier, whereas the outer planets (Jupiter, Saturn, Uranus, Neptune) are gassier.

The early Earth was a hot and dangerous place. It was bombarded by meteorites and asteroids, pressure heated the center as it grew larger and larger, and abundant radioactive materials added to the heat. Soon the young Earth was so hot that it melted in a process known as "differentiation." The heaviest elements, such as iron and nickel, sank to the center, where they formed the Earth's core. The metallic core generates the magnetic field that protects us from some of the more destructive forms of solar radiation. Lighter materials formed a squashy, semi-molten middle layer known as the "mantle." Even lighter materials stayed at the surface. These cooled more rapidly to form the eggshell-thin layer that we call the "crust." The crust is just a few kilometers deep. The lightest materials of all were the gases. These bubbled up through the Earth's volcanic surface to form the first atmosphere.

The first 500 million years of the Earth's history are known as the "Hadean" or "hellish" era. The Earth was hot, it was bombarded with asteroids, and its atmosphere contained no free oxygen. No living things could have survived. But slowly the Earth cooled. Eventually water vapor, circulating the Earth in vast clouds, began to rain down onto the surface to form the first oceans.

It was almost certainly in these early oceans that a new form of complexity began to appear: life. Water, in liquid form, provides a wonderful environment for chemical reactions. In air, atoms move past each other too fast to pair up. In solids, they barely move at all. Water is just right: chemicals move around but not too fast, so if they are compatible, they can pair up to start forming more complicated chemicals. Somewhere, probably deep in the early seas, where there was energy from deep-sea volcanoes and an abundance of chemicals, more and more complex chemicals began to form. By 3.5 billion years ago, within just a billion years of the Earth's creation, some of these chemicals formed the first living organisms. Biologists call these tiny, simple, one-celled organisms "prokaryotes," and prokaryotes remain the most common organisms on Earth even today. Like all prokaryotes, the first living organisms would have been too small to see. But they could do all the things that make living organisms so different from dead matter. They could take in energy from their surroundings using chemical reactions that biologists call "metabolism." They could also make copies of themselves, using the astonishing properties of the huge, complex molecules we call "DNA" (short for deoxyribonucleic acid). Prokaryotes reproduce simply by splitting into two nearly identical individuals, or "clones." There were always tiny inaccuracies in reproduction, however, which meant that there were tiny differences between individuals. Because of these differences, some individuals were slightly better at getting energy than others, and these tended to thrive and reproduce more successfully, passing on their abilities to their offspring as they did so. In this way living organisms gradually changed, adapting to a vast array of different environments and forming millions of distinct species. This is the process that Charles Darwin called "natural selection." It is the mechanism that has created the immense variety of living organisms that we observe today. As more and more species appeared, the Earth's surface was covered with a thin layer of life that we call the "biosphere." At present this is the only planet in the universe known to contain living organisms, but eventually it is mathematically probable that we will discover that life, in some form, exists in many other parts of the universe.

The first prokaryotes must have appeared by about 3.5 billion years ago because we have fossil traces of them. Through natural selection some of them had already discovered the trick of photosynthesis. That is the ability, present in all plants today, to extract energy directly from sunlight and store it inside their bodies. We know that photosynthesis began very early because of the existence of very ancient fossil "stromatolites," which are huge, coral-like objects built up from the bodies of millions of algae-like organisms and capable of photosynthesis. Photosynthesis has an important side-effect. The chemical reactions needed to extract energy from sunlight generate oxygen as a by-product. So, as the number of photosynthesizing organisms multiplied, more and more oxygen was pumped into the atmosphere. For some organisms this was a disaster because oxygen is extremely reactive and can be very destructive. If you doubt this, think of fire: fire is simply oxygen reacting with other elements. Indeed, geologists can track the slow build-up of free oxygen because they start finding bands of red iron that have combined with free oxygen in the slow form of burning that we call "rusting."

Some species, however, managed to adapt to the increasingly oxygen-rich atmosphere. And some began to use the high energy of oxygen atoms to power their own metabolism. In this way there appeared the first "eukaryotes," perhaps 2 billion years ago. The appearance of eukaryotes marks the appearance of a new level of complexity. Eukaryotes, like prokaryotes, were single-celled organisms. But they were mostly larger than prokaryotes, and they protected their DNA in a central nucleus. This ensured that they reproduced more accurately. Some also began to swap bits and pieces of DNA before reproducing, which meant that their offspring shared the qualities of both parents. This was the beginning of a new form of reproduction that we call "sexual reproduction." Sexual reproduction generates more variety because the offspring are never quite identical to either of their parents, and as a result, the pace of natural selection accelerated. That is why, during the last billion years of the Earth's history, the variety of types of living organisms seems to have increased more rapidly than ever before.

One of the most momentous of all changes in the history of our biosphere (along with the human-caused changes found in the "Anthropocene epoch" discussed in the final chapter) was the appearance, about 600 million years ago, of the first multi-celled organisms. In the Ediacaran era and then in the Cambrian era, there suddenly appear large fossils that can be seen with the naked eye. From then on, although most organisms still were single-celled prokaryotes or eukaryotes, paleontologists can trace the appearance of an increasing variety of multi-cellular organisms. Each of these organisms consisted of billions of eukaryotic cells that collaborated so closely together that they formed a single creature. Their appearance marks a new level of complexity.

At first all multi-celled organisms lived in the sea. But by 500 million years ago, some (probably early forms of plants or insects) began to explore the land. This was not easy because they had evolved in water and needed water to maintain their metabolism and to reproduce. So, like all of today's land organisms, they had to develop special skins to protect the complex chemical reactions taking place within their bodies and even more elaborate protective mechanisms for their offspring, such as eggs. Since then, millions of species of large organisms have appeared, flourished, and died out again, including the earliest amphibians, the dinosaurs, and the first mammals. We know, too, that there were periods of sudden change when thousands or millions of species were just wiped out. Sometimes these "extinction events" were caused by the collision of Earth with some of the asteroids that still cruise around our solar system. Such collisions would have been like nuclear wars. They would have created huge clouds of dust, obscuring the sun for months or years, as well as violent tsunamis. It was probably an asteroid impact that wiped out most species of dinosaurs about 65 million years ago. The earliest mammals were probably small, burrowing creatures a bit like shrews. Their small size and nocturnal habits may have helped them survive the terrors of an asteroid impact better than the larger dinosaurs.

With the dinosaurs out of the way, mammals began to adapt to the many environments that dinosaurs had occupied. So, quite rapidly we see the appearance of a large number of new mammal species. One group, the primates, lived mainly in trees. To do so, the primates needed hands that could grasp, eyes that were capable of stereoscopic vision, and large brains that were capable of processing plenty of visual information. Within the last 20 million years some primates, early forms of "apes," began to spend more time living on the ground. About 7 million years ago, somewhere in Africa, some apes began to stand on two legs. These were the first "hominines," bipedal apes that were our immediate ancestors.

Perhaps our most famous hominine ancestor is "Lucy." She belonged to the hominine group known as "Australopithecines" and lived about 3 million years ago in what is today Ethiopia in Africa. We can tell from the way her spine is attached to her skull that Lucy was bipedal. Mary Leakey, one of the pioneers of human paleontology, also discovered the fossilized footprints of two Australopithecines that had walked through the ash of a volcanic eruption. Lucy was smaller than us and had a brain about the size of that of a modern chimp, so, if we had met her we would have probably thought of her as a sort of chimp. Two million years ago, in east Africa, there appeared another hominine species, known as *Homo habilis*. What made this species different was that its members could manufacture simple stone tools. Within a half million years, there appeared another hominine species, *Homo ergaster,* or *Homo erectus* (paleontologists still argue about the exact terminology). Members of this species were about the same size as us and had brains almost as large as ours. They also made stone tools more sophisticated than those of *Homo habilis.* Some members of this species left Africa and migrated, over many generations, as far as China.

Our own species, *Homo sapiens,* appeared about 250,000 years ago, probably somewhere in east Africa. With our appearance we enter the domain of human history. As we will see, our appearance also marks the appearance of a new level of complexity, which is why human history is so different from the history of all other living species.

Beginnings: The Foraging Era

The era of foragers was the time in human history when all human communities lived by searching out or hunting food and other things they needed, rather than by growing or manufacturing them. Such people are also called "hunter-gatherers." This era is also known as the "Paleolithic era" (*Paleolithic* means "old Stone Age"). The era of foragers was the first and by far the longest era of human history. It was the time when the foundations of human history were laid down.

Foragers gather the resources they need for food, for shelter and clothing, and for ritual activities and other purposes. For the most part they do so without trying to transform their environment. The exceptional cultural and technological creativity of human foragers distinguishes their lifeways (the many different ways in which people relate to their environments and to each other) from the superficially similar lifeways of nonhuman species, such as the great apes. Only humans can communicate using symbolic language. Language allows men and women to share and accumulate knowledge in detail and with great precision. As a result of this constant sharing of knowledge, the skills and lifeways of ancient foragers gradually adapted to a huge variety of environments, creating a cultural and technological variety that has no parallel among any other large species. The extraordinary facility with which human communities adapted to new circumstances and environments is the key to human history.

As far as we know, the earliest human beings were foragers; thus, the era of foragers began about 250,000 years ago, when modern humans—members of our own species, *Homo sapiens*—first appeared on Earth. Although some foraging communities exist even today, the era of foragers ended about ten thousand years ago with the appearance of the first agricultural communities because after that time foraging ceased to be the only lifeway practiced by human societies.

10

⚔ Key Events in the Foraging Era ⚕

300,000–200,000 BCE	Modern human beings appear in Africa.
250,000 BCE	Stone tool technology becomes more sophisticated.
200,000 BCE	Humans begin spreading across Africa.
100,000 BCE	Humans begin migrating out of Africa to Eurasia.
50,000 BCE	Development of more sophisticated technologies accelerates.
	Large-scale extinction of many large land animals begins.
50,000–40,000 BCE	Australia is settled.
30,000 BCE	Siberia is settled.
30,000–20,000 BCE	More sophisticated tools such as the bow and arrow are invented.
13,000 BCE	Humans arrive in the Americas.
10,000 BCE	The foraging era ends with the development of agriculture.

All dates are approximate.

Studying the Era of Foragers

Historians have had a hard time integrating the era of foragers into their accounts of the past because most historians lack the research skills needed to study an era that generated no written evidence. Traditionally the era of foragers has been studied not by historians, but rather by archaeologists, anthropologists, and *pre*historians.

In the absence of written evidence scholars use three other fundamentally different types of evidence to understand the history of this era. The first type consists of physical remains from past societies. Archaeologists interpret, among other relics, bones and stones. They study the skeletal remains of humans and their prey species, leftover objects such as stone tools and other manufactured objects or the remains of meals, as well as evidence from the natural environment that may help them understand climatic and environmental changes. We have few skeletal remains for the earliest phases of human history; the earliest known skeletal remains that are definitely of modern humans date from around 160,000 years ago. Archaeologists, however, can extract a surprising amount of information from fragmentary skeletal remains. A close study of teeth, for example, can tell us much about diets, and diets can tell us much about the lifeways of early hu-

Topics for Further Study

Archaeology

Human Evolution

Human Genetics

Paleoanthropology

Paleolithic Art and Artifacts

mans. Similarly, differences in size between the skeletons of males and females can tell us something about gender relations. By studying fossilized pollens and core samples taken from seabeds and ice sheets that have built up during thousands of years, archaeologists have managed to reconstruct climatic and environmental changes with increasing precision. In addition, the dating techniques developed during the last fifty years have given us increasingly precise dates, which allow us to construct absolute chronologies of events during the entire span of human history.

Although archaeological evidence tells us mostly about the material life of our ancestors, it can occasionally give us tantalizing glimpses into their cultural and even spiritual lives. Particularly revealing are the astonishing artistic creations of early human communities, although precise interpretations of artifacts such as the great cave paintings of southern France and northern Spain remain beyond our grasp.

❧ Comparing the Three Eras ❧ of Human History

Era 1: Foraging	250,000– 8,000 BCE	Most of human history; small communities; global migrations; megafaunal extinctions; slow population growth
Era 2: Agrarian	8,000 BCE– 1750 CE	Intensification; rapid population growth; cities, states, empires; writing; different histories in different world zones
Era 3: Modern	1750– Present	Single, global system; rapid growth in energy use; increasing rate of extinctions; increased life expectancies

The second major type of evidence used to study early human history comes from studies of modern foraging communities. Such studies must be used with caution because modern foragers are modern; their lifeways are all influenced in varying degrees by the modern world. Nevertheless, by studying modern foraging lifeways, we can learn much about basic patterns of life in small foraging communities; thus, such studies have helped prehistorians interpret the meager material evidence available.

Recently a third type of evidence, based on comparative studies of modern genetic differences, has provided new ways of studying early human history. Genetic studies can determine degrees of genetic separation between modern populations and can help us estimate both the age of our species and the dates at which different populations were separated by ancient migrations.

Integrating these different types of evidence into a coherent account of world history is difficult not only because most historians lack the

Carbon Dating

The extract below underscores the revolutionary impact carbon dating has had on archaeology.

Carbon 14 (hereafter C 14) was developed by the American chemist, Willard F. Libby at the University of Chicago in the '50s, for which he received the Nobel Prize in Chemistry in 1960. C 14 dating provided an accurate means of dating a wide variety of organic material in most archaeological sites, and indeed in most environments throughout the world. The method revolutionized scientists' ability to date the past. It freed archaeologists from trying to use artifacts as their only means of determining chronologies, and it allowed them for the first time to apply the same absolute time scale uniformly from region to region and continent to continent. Many older archaeological schemes were overturned with the advent of C 14 dating. Today it is possible to date sites . . . well back into the late Pleistocene with reliable and accurate chronologies.

Source: Hudson, M. (n.d.). Understanding Carbon 14 dating. Retrieved May 16, 2007, from http://www.flmnh.ufl.edu/natsci/vertpaleo/aucilla10_1/Carbon.htm

necessary expertise and training, but also because archaeological, anthropological, and genetic evidence yields types of information that differ from the written sources that are the primary research base for most professional historians. Archaeological evidence from the era of foragers can never give us the intimate personal details that can be found in written sources, but it can tell us much about how people lived. Integrating the insights of these different disciplines is one of the main challenges of world history, and it is faced most directly in studying the era of foragers.

Beginnings of Human History

Scholars still debate when our species first appeared. One hypothesis—the multiregional model, defended today by a minority of physical anthropologists, including Milford Wolpoff and Alan Thorne—states that modern humans evolved gradually, during the last million years, in many regions of the Afro-Eurasian landmass. Through time protohumans (early human ancestors) in different regions diverged enough to create the genetic foundations for modern regional variants (races) while maintaining sufficient genetic contact to remain a single species. The multiregional model implies that human history began, quite gradually, sometime during the last million years. The evidence for this model comes mainly from the comparative study of skeletal remains.

Out of Africa, into Controversy

A second hypothesis, sometimes known as the "Out-of-Africa hypothesis," relies mainly on genetic comparisons of modern humans, although it also claims to be consistent with surviving skeletal evidence. It starts from the observation that modern humans are genetically very similar to each other, so similar in fact that they cannot have been evolving for more than about 250,000 years. This hypothesis suggests that all modern humans are descended from just a few ancestors who lived about 250,000 years ago. Today the greatest genetic variety among humans can be found in Africa, which suggests that Africa is where humans evolved and where they lived for the longest time before some began to migrate around the world. If the Out-of-Africa hypothesis is correct, modern humans evolved in Africa from later forms of a species known as *Homo ergaster* or *Homo erectus*. The new species probably emerged quite rapidly in a remote, isolated group.

The Out-of-Africa hypothesis itself comes in two main variants. The first variant, which has long been defended by the archaeologist Richard Klein and others, suggests that even if modern humans evolved in Africa perhaps 250,000 years ago, the earliest evidence of distinctively human behaviors, including improved hunting skills and artistic activities of various kinds, dates from no earlier than about fifty thousand to sixty thousand years ago. In this variant humans were not fully human, and human history did not really begin until some minor genetic changes made available the full range of modern symbolic languages. This variant of the Out-of-Africa hypothesis depends on the proliferation of new types of tools and artifacts that is evident in the archaeology of Eurasia from about fifty thousand years ago.

More recently, some supporters of the Out-of-Africa hypothesis have argued that the significance of these changes may have been exaggerated by virtue of the fact that scholars have conducted so much more archaeological research in Eurasia than in Africa, the presumed homeland of modern humans. In a careful analysis of the available archaeological evidence from Africa, the anthropologists Sally McBrearty and Alison Brooks have argued that evidence of distinctively human activities appears in Africa as early as 200,000 to 300,000 years ago and coincides with the appearance of skeletal remains that may be those of the earliest modern men and women. If McBrearty and Brooks are right, our species appeared in Africa between 200,000 and 300,000 years ago, and these dates mark the real beginnings of human history. The periodization adopted in *This Fleeting World* is based on these findings. It adopts the compromise date of 250,000 years ago for the appearance of the first humans and for the beginnings of human history. We should remember, however, that this date remains subject to revision.

WHAT MAKES US DIFFERENT?

What distinguishes us so markedly from other species? What distinguishes human history from the histories of all other animals? Many answers have been given to these fundamental questions. Modern answers include our ability to walk on two legs (bipedalism), our use of tools, our ability to hunt systematically, and our development of exceptionally large brains. Unfortunately, as studies of closely related species have become more sophisticated, we have learned that many of these qualities can be found to

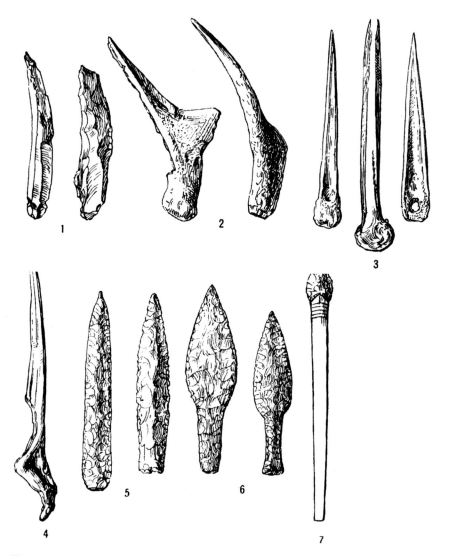

The plate shows a variety of early stabbing tools. Tools 1–2 are made from flaked stone. 2 from antler. 3 from animal bone. 4 from antler. 5 through 7 from chipped stone.

some degree in closely related species such as chimpanzees. For example, Jane Goodall, the first modern researcher to study chimpanzees in their native environments, learned very soon that chimpanzees can make and use tools and can also hunt.

Topics for Further Study

Animism

Creation Myths

Development of Language

At the moment the most powerful marker, the feature that distinguishes our species most decisively from closely related species, appears to be symbolic language. Many animals can communicate with each other and share information in rudimentary ways. But humans are the only creatures who can communicate using symbolic language: a system of arbitrary symbols that can be linked by formal grammars to create a nearly limitless variety of precise utterances. Symbolic language greatly enhanced the precision of human communication and the range of ideas that humans can exchange. Symbolic language allowed people for the first time to talk about entities that were not immediately present (including experiences and events in the past and future) as well as entities whose existence was not certain (such as souls, demons, and dreams).

The result of this sudden increase in the precision, efficiency, and range of human communication systems was that people could share much more of what they learned with others; thus, knowledge began to accumulate more rapidly than it was lost. Instead of dying with each person or generation, the insights of individuals could be preserved for future generations.

As a result, each generation inherited the accumulated knowledge of previous generations, and, as this store of knowledge grew, later generations could use it to adapt to their environment in new ways. Unlike all other living species on Earth, whose behaviors change in significant ways only when the genetic makeup of the entire species changes, humans can change their behaviors significantly without waiting for their genes to change. This cumulative process of "collective learning" explains the exceptional ability of humans to adapt to changing environments and changing circumstances. It also explains the unique dynamism of human history. In human history culture has overtaken natural selection as the primary motor of change.

These conclusions suggest that we should seek the beginnings of human history not only in the anatomical details of early human remains, but also in any evidence that hints at the presence of symbolic language and the accumulation of technical skills. The findings of McBrearty and Brooks link the earliest evidence of symbolic activity (including hints of the grinding of pigments for use in body painting) and of significant changes in stone

---

Thought Experiment

Most people are not conscious of how human communication systems have an impact on every aspect of our lives. Consider the route between your home and your school and what you know and think about the things you see along the way. Now ask yourself: "How many of the thoughts and ideas in my head were NOT put there by some other human being, either through speech or writing? How many of the objects I use every day could I invent without the help of other humans?" This may remind you of how much we depend on the thoughts and experiences of other human beings.

---

tool technologies (including the disappearance of the stone technologies associated with most forms of *Homo ergaster*) with the appearance of a new species known as "*Homo helmei.*" The remains of this species are so close to those of modern women and men that we may eventually have to classify them with our own species, *Homo sapiens.* The earliest anatomical, technological, and cultural evidence for these changes appears in Africa between 200,000 and 300,000 years ago.

Foraging Lifeways

Archaeological evidence is so scarce for the era of foragers that our understanding of early human lifeways has been shaped largely by conclusions based on the study of modern foraging communities. Indeed, the notion of a foraging mode of production was first proposed by the anthropologist Richard Lee during the late 1970s on the basis of his studies of foraging communities in southern Africa. However, the scanty archaeological evidence can be used to discipline the generalizations suggested by modern anthropological research.

The scarcity of remains from the foraging era, combined with what we know of the lifeways and technologies of modern foragers, makes us certain that levels of productivity were extraordinarily low by modern standards. Humans probably did not extract from their environment much more than the 3,000 kilocalories per day that adult members of our species need to maintain a basic, healthy existence.

Low productivity ensured that population densities were low by the standards of later eras, averaging perhaps as little as one person per square kilometer. This fact meant that small numbers of humans were scattered over large ranges.

Modern studies suggest that foragers may have deliberately limited population growth to avoid overexploitation of the land. Modern studies have also shown that foragers can limit population growth by inhibiting conception through prolonged breast feeding, by using various techniques of abortion, and sometimes by killing excess children or allowing the sick, aged, and unhealthy to die.

Because each group needed a large area to support itself, ancient foragers, like modern foragers, probably lived most of the time in small groups consisting of no more than a few closely related people. Most of these groups must have been nomadic. You had to walk a lot in order to exploit a large home territory! We can also be sure that many links existed between neighboring groups, however. Almost all human communities encourage marriage away from one's immediate family. Thus, foraging communities likely met periodically with their neighbors to swap gifts, stories, and rituals, to dance together, and to resolve disputes. At such meetings—similar, perhaps, to the corroborees of Aboriginal Australians—females and males may have moved from group to group either spontaneously or through more formal arrangements of marriage or adoption.

KITH AND KIN

Exchanges of people meant that each group normally had family members in neighboring groups, creating ties that ensured that people usually had some sense of solidarity between neighboring groups as well as some linguistic overlapping. Ties of kinship created local networks that smoothed the exchange of goods, people, and ideas between neighboring groups.

Studies of modern foraging societies suggest that notions of family and kinship provided the primary way of thinking about and organizing social relations. Indeed, in *Europe and the People without History* (1982), the anthropologist Eric Wolf proposed describing all small-scale societies as "kin-ordered." Family *was* society in a way that is difficult for the inhabitants of modern societies to appreciate. Notions of kinship provided all the rules of behavior and etiquette that were needed to live in a world in which most communities included just a few persons and in which few people met more than a few hundred other people in their lifetime.

The idea of society as family also suggests much about the economics of foraging societies. Relations of exchange were probably analogous to those in modern families. Exchanges were conceived of as gifts. This fact meant that the act of exchanging was usually more important than the qualities of the goods exchanged; exchanging was a way of cementing existing relationships. Anthropologists say that such relationships are based on "reciprocity." Power relations, too, were the power relations of families or extended families; justice and discipline—even violent retribution for antisocial behavior—could be imposed only by the family. Hierarchies, insofar as they existed, were based on gender, age, experience, and respect within the family.

Studies of modern foraging societies suggest that, although males and females, just like older and younger members of society, may have specialized in different tasks, differences in the roles people played did not necessarily create hierarchical relations. Women probably took most responsibility for child rearing and may also have been responsible for gathering most of the food (at least in temperate and tropical regions, where gathering was more important than hunting), whereas men specialized in hunting, which was generally a less reliable source of food in such regions. No evidence indicates that these different roles led to relationships of dominance or subordination, however. Throughout the era of foragers human relationships were personal rather than hierarchical. In a world of intimate, personal relationships people had little need for the highly institutionalized structures of the modern world, most of which are designed to regulate relationships between strangers.

Burials and art objects of many kinds have left us tantalizing hints about the spiritual world of our foraging ancestors but few definitive answers. Modern analogies suggest that foragers thought of the spiritual world and the natural world as parts of a large extended family, full of beings with whom one could establish relations of kinship, mutual obligation, and sometimes enmity. As a result, the classificatory boundaries that foragers drew between human beings and all

Topics for Further Study

Foraging Societies

Indigenous Peoples

Kinship

Marriage and Family

other species and entities were less hard and fast than those we draw today. Such thinking may help make sense of ideas that often seem bizarre to moderns, such as totemism—the idea that animals, plants, and even natural geological objects such as mountains and lakes can be thought of as kin. The belief that all or most of reality is animated by spirit may be the fundamental cosmological hypothesis (or model of the universe) of foraging societies, even if particular representations of spirits differ greatly from community to community. The hypothesis helped make sense of a world in which animals and objects often behave with all the unpredictability and willfulness of human beings.

LIVING STANDARDS

In an article published in 1972 the anthropologist Marshall Sahlins questioned the conventional assumption that material living standards were necessarily low in foraging societies. He argued, mainly on the basis of

Thought Experiment

The diets of early foragers were very different from ours, but the dietary needs of early foragers were similar to ours. Consider how fast we can rack up 3,000 kcal today. You could do it with a modern-day fast-food diet like this:

Breakfast Dunkin' Donuts sausage, egg, and cheese croissant (690 kcal), hot chocolate (220 kcal)

Lunch McDonald's McChicken sandwich (425 kcal), with a 16-oz. cola (210 kcal), 10 onion rings (244 kcal)

Dinner A Burger King Whopper (670 kcal), a medium shake (560 kcal)

Now imagine how long it would take you to get that many calories if there were no shops and you had to get them all from fruit, grubs, fish, and other things you could find in the environment around your home? How much of your day would you spend doing this? How much new knowledge would you need in order to know what foods were safe to eat, and where you could find good food?

evidence from modern foragers, that from some points of view we could view foragers (certainly those living in less harsh environments) as affluent. Nomadism discouraged the accumulation of material goods because people had to carry everything they owned; so did a lifeway in which people took most of what they needed from their immediate surroundings. In such a world people had no need to accumulate material possessions. Absence of possessions may seem a mark of poverty to modern minds, but Sahlins argued that foragers probably experienced their lives as affluent because the things they needed could be found all around them. Particularly in temperate regions, the diets of foragers can be varied and nutritious; indeed, the variety of the diets of ancient foragers shielded them from famine because when their favorite foodstuffs failed, they had many alternatives to fall back on.

LEISURELY BUT BRIEF

Studies by paleobiologists (paleontologists who study the biology of fossil organisms) have confirmed that the health of foragers was often better than that of people in the earliest farming communities. The small communities in which foragers lived insulated them from epidemic diseases, and frequent movement prevented the accumulation of rubbish that could attract disease-carrying pests. Modern analogies suggest that they also lived a life of considerable leisure, rarely spending more than a few hours a day in pursuit of the basic necessities of life—far less than most people either in farming communities or in modern societies. We should not exaggerate, however. In other ways life was undeniably harsh during the era of foragers. For example, life expectancies were probably low (perhaps less than thirty years). Although many persons undoubtedly lived into their sixties or seventies, high rates of infant mortality, physical accidents, and interpersonal violence took a greater toll from the young in foraging societies than in most modern societies

Major Changes during the Era of Foragers

The small size of foraging communities and the limited possibilities for exchanging ideas over large areas may explain why, to modern minds, technological change during this era appears to have been so slow. Nevertheless, change was extremely rapid in comparison with the changes that

Thought Experiment

Look around the classroom. Consider that if you had lived in the era of foragers, you wouldn't have had to go to school, you would never have been inside a square-shaped room, and you'd probably all be outside searching for nuts, berries, or deer. Well, maybe not all of you. At least half would no longer be alive, because about 50 percent of children died by the age of ten. If you were one of the lucky ones to have survived, imagine how it would feel to lose siblings so often and so young.

took place among our hominid (erect bipedal primate mammals comprising recent humans and extinct ancestral and related forms) ancestors or among other large animal species. To give just one example, the Acheulian hand axes (a type of stone tool originating in Africa almost 2 million years ago) used by our immediate ancestors, *Homo ergaster,* changed little during a million and more years. Yet, during the 200,000 years or more of the era of foragers, our ancestors created a remarkable variety of new technologies and new lifeways. Indeed, the relatively sudden replacement of Acheulian stone technologies by more varied and precisely engineered stone tools in Africa from about 200,000 years ago is one of the most powerful reasons for thinking that modern humans existed by that date. Many of these new stone tools were so small that they may have been hafted (bound to handles), which would have greatly increased their versatility and usefulness.

The technological creativity of our foraging ancestors enabled them to explore and settle lands quite different from those in which they had evolved. Indeed, this creativity is one of the most decisive differences between our species and other species, including our closest relatives, the great apes. As far as we know, the great apes have not managed to modify their behaviors enough to migrate into new habitats. This fact is precisely why we do not customarily think of these species as having histories in the way that humans have a history. In contrast, the history of our species during the era of foragers is a story of many unrecorded migrations into new environments, made possible by tiny technological changes, the accumulation of new knowledge and skills, and minor adjustments in lifeways.

As humans spread over more and more of the Earth, human numbers surely increased. Estimates of populations during the era of foragers are based largely on guesswork, though genetic evidence suggests that human numbers shrank to just a few thousands about 70,000 years ago. One of the more influential recent estimates by demographer Massimo Livi-Bacci suggests that thirty thousand years ago there were a few hundred thousand humans, but by ten thousand years ago there may have been as many as 6 million. If we assume that approximately 500,000 humans existed thirty thousand years ago, this implies a growth rate between thirty thousand and ten thousand years ago of less than 0.01 percent per annum, which implies that human populations were doubling approximately every eight thousand to nine thousand years. This rate of growth can be compared with an average doubling time of about fourteen hundred years during the agrarian era and eighty-five years during the modern era.

TECHNOLOGICAL CHANGE

Rates of growth during the era of foragers are striking in two contradictory ways. Insofar as population growth is an indirect sign of technological innovation, it provides evidence for innovation throughout the era and some signs that innovation was accelerating. By comparison with later eras of

Thought Experiment

What does the "doubling time" of a population really mean? Consider the population growth rate of 0.01 percent per year—which is the assumption made for the populations of thirty thousand years ago. To understand what doubling time at this growth rate would mean, imagine this scenario: there is a village of eleven people, just enough for a soccer team. But they would like to play another team, and they don't know of any other humans. At this rate of reproduction how long would they have to wait before there are twenty-two people around? Answer: nine thousand years. (More if they think there are going to have to be substitutes!)

human history, however, rates of growth were extremely slow. This difference is partly because exchanges of information were limited by the small size and the wide dispersion of foraging communities. Indeed, change occurred so slowly that a person could hardly notice it within a single lifetime, and this fact may mean that ancient foragers had little sense of long-term change, seeing the past mainly as a series of variations on the present.

Migrations into new environments requiring new technologies and new skills probably began quite early during the era of foragers, while all humans still lived within the African continent. Unfortunately, studying technological change during the earliest stages of human history is difficult because surviving objects tell us little about the technological knowledge of those who made them. Today we depend upon objects such as cars and computers, which embody a colossal amount of specialized knowledge. Modern anthropological studies suggest, however, that among foragers knowledge was primarily carried in the head rather than embodied in objects. Thus, the tools that foragers left behind can give us only the palest impression of their technological and ecological skills.

Nevertheless, the evidence of change is powerful. The first piece of evidence that humans were migrating into new environments is the fact that human remains start appearing in all parts of the African continent. By 100,000 years ago some groups had learned to live off the resources

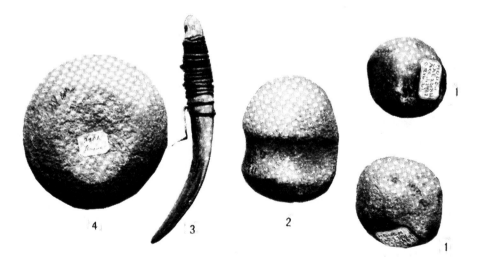

This plate shows a variety of early tools used to flake or abrade stone.

of seashore environments, such as shellfish, whereas others were adapting to lifeways in tropical forests and deserts. Evidence that communities exchanged objects over distances up to several hundred kilometers suggests that communities were also exchanging information over considerable distances, and these exchanges may have been a vital stimulus to technological experimentation.

MIGRATIONS FROM AFRICA

From about 100,000 years ago some humans began to settle outside Africa. Communities of modern humans appeared in southwestern Asia, and from there humans migrated west and east to the southern, and warmer, parts of the Eurasian landmass. These migrations took humans into environments similar to those of their African homeland, so they do not necessarily indicate any technological breakthroughs. Indeed, many other species had made similar migrations between Asia and Africa. The appearance of humans in ice age Australia by forty thousand to fifty thousand years ago, however, is a clear sign of innovation because traveling to Australia demanded sophisticated seagoing capabilities, and within Australia humans had to adapt to an entirely novel biological realm. We know of no other mammal species that made this crossing independently.

Equally significant is the appearance of humans in Siberia from about thirty thousand years ago. To live in the steppes (vast, usually level and treeless tracts) of Inner Asia during the last ice age, you had to be extremely good at hunting large mammals such as deer, horse, and mammoth because edible plants were scarcer than in warmer climates. You also had to be able to protect yourself from the extreme cold by using fire, making close-fitting clothes, and building durable shelters. By thirteen thousand years ago humans had also reached the Americas, traveling either across the ice age land bridge of Beringia, which linked eastern Siberia and Alaska, or by sea around the coasts of Beringia. Within two thousand years of entering the Americas, some groups had reached the far south of South America.

Each of these migrations required new technologies, new botanical and biological knowledge, and new ways of

Topics for Further Study

Extinctions

Migrations in Afro-Eurasia, Asia, and Europe

Population Growth

Technology

Thought Experiment

If your community moved an average of just ten miles (sixteen kilometers) a year, consider how many years would it take to travel from Africa through Russia and Siberia, to Alaska and then down through the Americas to Tierra del Fuego? Migrations needed advances in technology to be successful. Then imagine what new knowledge you would need as you traveled from Africa (with its warm climates and abundant vegetation and animal life), to Siberia (with cold climates, scarce vegetation but lots of large animals such as mammoth), to North America (with its huge forests and unfamiliar animals and plants), through the tropical lands of Central America and then through the Andes to Tierra del Fuego?

---

living; thus, each represents a technological breakthrough, within which numerous lesser technological adjustments took place as communities learned to exploit the particular resources of each microregion. No evidence indicates that the average size of human communities increased, however. During the era of foragers technological change led to more extensive rather than more intensive settlement; humans settled more of the world, but they continued to live in small nomadic communities.

HUMAN IMPACTS ON THE ENVIRONMENT

The technological creativity that made these migrations possible ensured that, although foragers normally had a limited impact on their environments, their impact was increasing. The extinction of many large animal species (megafauna) and the spread of what is known as "fire-stick farming" provide two spectacular illustrations of the increasing human impact on the environment, although controversy still surrounds both topics.

Megafaunal Extinctions

Within the last fifty thousand years many species of large animals have been driven to extinction, particularly in regions newly colonized by humans, whether in Australia, Siberia, or the Americas. Australia and the Americas may have lost 70–80 percent of all mammal species weighing more than 100 pounds (45 kilograms). These species included giant kangaroos and wombats in Australia, mammoth and wooly rhinos in ice age Siberia, horses, camels, giant sloths and saber-toothed tigers in the Americas. Europe may have lost 40 percent of large-animal species; whereas Africa, where humans and large mammals had co-existed for much longer, lost only about 14 percent. As archaeologists pinpoint the date of these extinctions more precisely, the extinctions appear to coincide with the first arrival of modern humans, increasing the probability that they were *caused* by humans.

Similar extinctions during recent centuries, such as the extinction of the ostrich-sized birds known as "moas" in New Zealand, offer a modern example of what may have happened as humans with improved hunting techniques and skills encountered large animals who had little experience of humans and whose low reproduction rates made them particularly vulnerable to extinction. The loss of large-animal species in Australia and the Americas shaped the later histories of these regions because the lack of large animals meant that humans were unable to exploit large animals as beasts of burden and sources of foodstuffs and fibers.

Fire-Stick Farming

A second example of the increasing environmental impact of early foragers is associated with what the Australian archaeologist Rhys Jones called "fire-stick farming." Fire-stick farming is not, strictly, a form of farming at all. However, it is, like farming, a way of manipulating the environment to increase the productivity of animal and plant species that humans find useful. Fire-stick farmers regularly burn off the land to prevent the accumulation of dangerous amounts of fuel. Regular firing also clears undergrowth and deposits ash. In effect, it speeds up the decomposition of dead organisms, which encourages the growth of new shoots that can attract grazing animals and the animals that prey on them. Within days or weeks, hunters could return to the land they had fired and expect to find many new plants as well as lots of animals grazing them.

Humans systematically fired the land on all the continents they settled, and through time the practice probably transformed local landscapes and altered the mix of local animal and plant species. In Australia, for example, fire-stick farming through tens of thousands of years probably encouraged the spread of eucalyptus at the expense of species that were less comfortable with fire, creating landscapes very different from those encountered by the earliest human immigrants.

PICKING UP THE PACE

From about fifty thousand years ago the rate of technological change began to accelerate. Migrations to new continents and new environments are one sign of acceleration. New technologies and techniques also proliferated, however. Stone tools became more precise and more varied, and many may have been hafted. People began to use new materials such as bone, amber, and vegetable fibers. From about thirty thousand to twenty thousand years ago, new and more sophisticated tools appeared, including bows and arrows and spear throwers.

Foragers in tundra (level or rolling treeless plain that is characteristic of arctic and subarctic regions) regions used bone needles to make carefully tailored clothes from animal skins; sometimes they covered their clothing with elaborate ornamentation made from animal teeth or shells. The remains of prey species show that hunters, particularly in cold climates, became more specialized in their hunting techniques, which suggests that their understanding of different environments was becoming more and more sophisticated. Cave paintings and sculptures in wood or bone began to appear in regions as disparate as Africa, Australia, Mongolia, and Europe.

AFFLUENT FORAGERS

Accelerating technological change accounts for one more development that foreshadowed the changes that would eventually lead to the agrarian era. Most foraging technologies can be described as "extensive." They allowed humans to occupy larger areas without increasing the size of individual communities. Occasionally, though, foragers adopted more intensive techniques, that is to say techniques that allowed them to extract more resources from a given area. This allowed them to create larger and more sedentary (settled) communities. Evidence for such changes is particularly common from about twenty thousand to fifteen thousand years ago and is best known from the corridor between Mesopotamia (the region of southwestern Asia between the Tigris and Euphrates Rivers) and the Nile Valley—the region that links Africa and Eurasia. Anthropologists have long been aware that foragers living in environments of particular abundance will sometimes become less nomadic and spend longer periods at one or

This illustration depicts designs on a large Tsimshian box used to store blankets, an important form of wealth for affluent foragers.

two main home bases. They may also become more sedentary if they devise technologies that increase the output of resources from a particular area. Anthropologists refer to such foragers as "affluent foragers."

The examples that follow are taken from Australia, where foraging life-ways can be studied more closely because they have survived into modern times. During the last five thousand years new, smaller, and more finely made stone tools appeared in many parts of Australia, including small points that people may have used as spear tips. Some tools were so beautifully made that they were traded as ritual objects over hundreds of miles. New techniques meant new ways of extracting resources. In the state of Victoria people built elaborate eel traps, some with canals up to 300 meters long. At certain points people constructed nets or tapered traps, using bark strips or plaited rushes, to harvest the trapped eels. So many eels could be kept in these "eel farms" that relatively permanent settlements appeared nearby. One site contains almost 150 small huts built of stone. In addition to eels, the inhabitants of these small settlements lived off local species of game, from emu to kanga-roo, as well as local vegetable foods such as daisy yam tubers, ferns, and convolvulus (herbs and shrubs of the morning glory family).

Some communities began to harvest plants such as yams, fruit, and grains in ways that suggest early steps toward agriculture. Yams were (and are today) harvested in ways that encouraged re-growth, and people deliberately planted fruit seeds in refuse heaps to create fruit groves. In some of the more arid areas of central Australia, early European travelers observed communities harvesting wild millet with stone knives and storing it in large haystacks. Archaeologists have discovered grindstones that were used to grind seeds as early as fifteen thousand years ago in some regions. In many coastal regions of Australia people fished using shell hooks and small boats, and fishing enabled them to live in denser and more populous communities. In general, the coasts were more thickly settled than inland areas.

The appearance of communities of affluent foragers prepared the way for the next fundamental transition in human history: the appearance of communities that systematically manipulated their environments to extract more resources from a given area. The set of technologies that these people used is often called "agriculture"; we refer to the era in which agriculture was the most important basic technology as the "agrarian era."

The Era of Foragers in World History

Historians have often assumed that little changed during the long era of foragers. In comparison with later eras of human history this assumption may seem to be true. It is also true that change was normally so slow that it was imperceptible within a single lifetime; thus, few men and women in the era of foragers could have appreciated the wider significance of technological changes. Nevertheless, in comparison with the pace during the prehuman era, the pace of technological change during the era of foragers was striking. Exploiting the technological synergy (the creative power generated by linking people through language) that was made available to humans by their capacity for symbolic language, human communities slowly learned to live successfully in a wide variety of new environments. A gradual accumulation of new skills allowed foraging communities to settle most of the world in migrations that had no precedent either among other primate species or among our hominid ancestors.

During the course of 250,000 years the pace of change was slowly accelerating. During the last fifty thousand years or so, the variety and precision of foraging technologies and techniques multiplied throughout the world. Eventually foraging technologies became sophisticated enough to allow groups of people in some regions to exploit their surroundings more intensively, a change that marks the first step toward agriculture.

Acceleration: The Agrarian Era

T he agrarian era began ten thousand to eleven thousand years ago with the appearance of the first agricultural communities. We can define the agrarian era as "the era of human history when agriculture was the most important of all productive technologies and the foundation for most human societies." It ended during the last 250 years as modern industrial technologies overtook agriculture in productivity and began to transform human lifeways.

Although the agrarian era lasted a mere ten thousand years, in contrast to the 250,000 years of the era of foragers, 70 percent of all humanity may have lived during the agrarian era, because the technologies of this era were so much more productive than those of the era of foragers.

The agrarian era was characterized by greater diversity than either the era of foragers or the modern era. Paradoxically, diversity was a product both of technological innovations and of technological sluggishness because, although new technologies such as agriculture and pastoralism (livestock raising) created new ways of living, the limits of communications technologies ensured that different parts of the world remained separate enough to evolve along independent trajectories. We can identify several distinct "world zones." These were large regions that had no significant contact with each other before about 1500 CE. The four most important world zones were the Afro-Eurasian landmass (which stretched from the far south of Africa to the far northeast of Siberia), the Americas, Australia, and the islands of the Pacific.

Within each world zone long and sometimes tenuous webs of cultural and material exchanges linked local communities into larger networks of exchanges. In some of the world zones the dense networks of political, cultural, and economic exchanges known as "agrarian civilizations" emerged, and through time these civilizations linked with other agrarian civilizations and with peoples living between the main zones of agrarian civilization. We know of no significant contacts between the different world zones before 1492 CE, however. The great diversity of lifeways and the relative isolation of different regions explain why we have more difficulty making generalizations that apply to the entire world during this era than during the era of foragers or the modern era.

Still, there are some striking parallels between the historical trajectories of different parts of the world. Agriculture appeared quite independently in several regions; so did states, cities, monumental architecture, and writing. These parallels raise deep questions about long-term patterns of historical change. Does human history have a fundamental shape, a large trajectory that is apparent in all regions and under diverse social and ecological conditions? If such a shape exists, does it arise from the nature of our species or from basic principles of cultural evolution? Or are the similarities misleading? Should we be emphasizing the diversity and open-endedness of human historical experience rather than these larger patterns and commonalities?

Origins of Agriculture

The word *agriculture* is used here to describe an evolving cluster of technologies that enabled humans to increase the production of favored plant and animal species. Ecologically speaking, agriculture is a more efficient way than foraging to harvest the energy and resources stored in the natural environment as a result of photosynthesis. Because farmers interfere with their surroundings more deliberately than foragers, agriculture magnified

Thought Experiment

Imagine you were starting life after a disaster. You can't get to stores because there's no working transportation or communication. All you have to eat is what you can find in the woods or fields. What things do you know of within walking distance that you could eat safely? How would you cook them, and if you couldn't cook, how would you feel about chewing on raw fish and wild grain? Say you want to start growing your own food. Where would you start?

the human impact on the natural environment and also on the cultures and lifeways of humans themselves. Agriculturalists manipulated plant and animal species so intensely that they began to alter the genetic makeup of prey species in a process commonly referred to as "domestication." By clearing forests, diverting rivers, terracing hillsides, and plowing the land, agriculturalists created landscapes that were increasingly anthropogenic (shaped by human activity).

Finally, by altering their own lifeways, agriculturalists created new types of communities, radically different in scale and complexity from those of the era of foragers. Humans did not domesticate just other species; they also domesticated themselves.

Agriculture does not automatically increase the biological productivity of the land. Indeed, agriculturalists often reduce total productivity by removing the many species for which they have no use. They increase the productivity only of those plants and animals that they find most useful. Removing undesired plants leaves more nutrients, sunlight, and water for domesticated crops such as corn, wheat, or rice, while killing wolves and foxes allows cattle, sheep, and chickens to flourish in safety. By increasing the productivity of favored prey species, humans could feed more of themselves from a given area than would have been possible using foraging technologies.

Whereas technological change during the era of foragers was extensive (it allowed humans to multiply by increasing their range), technological change during the agrarian era was intensive (it allowed more humans to live within a given range). As a result, humans and their domesticates began to settle in larger and denser communities; as they did so they transformed their ecological and social environments. The result was a revolution in the pace and nature of historical change.

EARLIEST EVIDENCE OF AGRICULTURE

Dates for the earliest evidence of agriculture remain subject to revision. At present the earliest clear evidence comes from the corridor between the Nile Valley and Mesopotamia that links Africa and Eurasia. In the Fertile Crescent (the arc of highlands around the great rivers of Mesopotamia) grain crops were cultivated from about 8000 BCE (ten thousand years ago). In the Sahara Desert west of the Nile River, in lands that then were much less arid than they are today, communities may have domesticated cattle as

❧ Key Events in the Agrarian Era ❧

13000–11000 BCE	Some humans begin to live in settled communities.
9000–8000 BCE	Cattle are domesticated in the Sahara region of Africa.
8000 BCE	Grain crops are cultivated in Mesopotamia.
	Yams are cultivated in West Africa.
7000 BCE	Grains and rice are cultivated in the north and south of China.
	Yams and taro are cultivated in Papua New Guinea.
	Squash is cultivated in Mesoamerica.
4000 BCE	The secondary products revolution takes place in parts of Afro-Eurasia.
3000 BCE	Plants are cultivated in the Andes region of South America.
	Cities and states appear in Mesopotamia and Egypt.
2500 BCE	Cities and states appear in India, Pakistan, and northern China.
2000 BCE	Eurasian trade networks develop.
1000 BCE	Cities and states appear in Mesoamerica and the Andes.
500 BCE–1000 CE	New cities and states emerge, population increases, and interregional trade networks develop.
500–1200 CE	Many of the Pacific islands are settled.
1500 CE	All major world regions are linked through migration and trade.
1750 CE	The agrarian era ends with the appearance and spread of industrialization.

early as 9000 or 8000 BCE, and within a thousand years these same communities may have started cultivating sorghum. In west Africa yam cultivation may also have begun around 8000 BCE. In China people were probably cultivating rice in the south and other grains in the north by 7000 BCE. By this time farming based on the cultivation of taro (a large-leaved tropical Asian plant) and yam evidently existed in Papua New Guinea in the

Malay Archipelago. Communities probably farmed root crops early in many coastal regions in the tropics, although most traces of such communities would have been submerged as sea levels rose at the end of the last ice age. In Mesoamerica (the region including Mexico and much of the peninsula to its south) people probably domesticated squash

as early as 7000 BCE, but clearer evidence of systematic agriculture does not appear before 5000 BCE. In the Andes region the earliest evidence of agriculture appears after about 3000 BCE. From these and perhaps a few other regions in which agriculture appeared quite independently, agricultural technologies and ways of life eventually spread to most of the world.

At present we lack a fully satisfactory explanation for the origins of agriculture. Any explanation must account for the curious fact that, after 200,000 years or more during which all humans lived as foragers, agricultural lifeways appeared within just a few thousand years in parts of the world that had no significant contact with each other. The realization that agriculture arose quite independently in different parts of the world has undermined the once-fashionable view that agriculture was a brilliant invention that diffused from a single center as soon as people understood its benefits. That view was also undermined after researchers realized that foragers who know about agriculture have often preferred to remain foragers. Perhaps foragers resisted change because the health and nutritional levels of the first farmers were often lower than those of neighboring foragers, whereas their stress levels were often higher. If agriculture depressed living standards, then an explanation of the origins of agriculture must rely more on "push" than on "pull" factors. Rather than taking up agriculture willingly, we must assume that many early agriculturalists were *forced* to take it up.

AFFLUENT FORAGERS

The outlines of an explanation for the agricultural revolution are now available, even if many details remain to be tested in particular instances. The origins of agriculture have been studied most thoroughly in Mesopotamia and in Mesoamerica. In both areas the first agricultural villages appeared after many centuries during which foragers intensified their exploitation of particular favored resources, adapting their tools and techniques with increasing precision and efficiency to local environments. This was the first step toward agriculture. When taken far enough, such techniques can turn conventional foragers into "affluent foragers." Affluent foragers extract more resources from a given area than do traditional foragers. Eventually they may extract enough resources to become semisedentary, living in one place for much of the year. This development is particularly likely where prey resources such as fish or wild grains are unusually abundant. The appearance of such communities in many parts of the world toward the end of the last ice age tempts us to link such changes with the erratic global warming that began eighteen thousand to sixteen thousand years ago.

In both temperate and tropical zones warmer climates may have created local "gardens of Eden"—regions of exceptional abundance—where highly nutritious plants such as wild wheats that had once been scarce

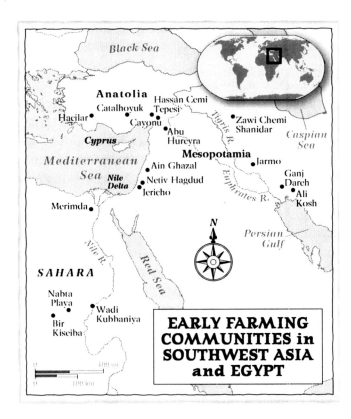

EARLY FARMING COMMUNITIES in SOUTHWEST ASIA and EGYPT

thrived and spread. Indeed, intensive agriculture may have been impossible under the harsh conditions of the last ice age; if so, the end of the last ice age was a crucial enabling feature, making agriculture possible for the first time in perhaps 100,000 years.

The end of the last ice age also coincided with the final stages of the great global migrations of the era of foragers. As the anthropologist Mark Cohen has pointed out, by the end of the last ice age few parts of the world were unoccupied, and by the standards of foragers some parts of the world may have seemed overpopulated. Perhaps the coincidence of warmer, wetter, and more productive climates with increasing population pressure in some regions explains why, in several parts of the world, beginning ten thousand to eleven thousand years ago, some communities of foragers began to settle down. The classic example of this change comes from the Natufian communities of the fertile highlands around Mesopotamia fourteen thousand to twelve thousand years ago. Natufian communities were largely sedentary but lived as foragers, harvesting wild grains and gazelle. Similar communities, harvesting wild sorghum, may have existed even earlier in modern Ethiopia, east of the Nile River.

FULL-BLOWN AGRICULTURE

Eventually some sedentary or semisedentary foragers became agriculturalists. The best explanation for this second stage in the emergence of agriculture may be demographic. As mentioned earlier, modern studies of nomadic foragers suggest that they can systematically limit population growth through prolonged breast feeding (which inhibits ovulation) and other practices, including infanticide and senilicide (killing of the very young and the very old, respectively). In sedentary communities living in regions of ecological abundance, however, such restraints were no longer necessary and may have been relaxed. If so, then within just two or three generations sedentary foraging communities that had lived in regions of abundance for a generation or two may have found that quite quickly they began to outgrow the resources available in their environment.

Overpopulation would have posed a clear choice: migrate or intensify (produce more food from the same area). Where land was scarce and neighboring

Topics for Further Study

Agricultural Societies

Secondary-products Revolution

Water Management

communities were also feeling the pinch, there may have been no choice at all. Sedentary foragers had to intensify. However, even those foragers able to return to their traditional, nomadic lifeways may have found that in just a few generations they had lost access to the lands used by their foraging ancestors and had also lost their traditional skills as nomadic foragers. Those communities that chose to intensify had to apply already-existing skills to the task of increasing productivity. They already had much of the knowledge they needed. They knew how to weed, how to water plants, and how to tame prey species of animals. The stimulus to apply such knowledge more precisely and more systematically was provided by over-population. Global warming at the end of the last ice age was what made intensification *possible* by increasing the range and productivity of many edible crops such as wheat and wild rice.

These arguments appear to explain the curious near-simultaneity of the transition to agriculture at the end of the last ice age. They also fit what is known of the transition to agriculture in several regions, particularly temperate regions where agriculture was based primarily on grains. They also help explain why, even in regions where developed agriculture did not appear, such as Australia, many of the preliminary steps toward agriculture do show up in the archaeological record, including the appearance of affluent, semisedentary foragers.

Seeds of Change

After agriculture had appeared in any one region, it spread, primarily because the populations of farming communities grew so fast that they had

Worth Debating

Warmer, wetter, and more productive climates after the last ice age may explain why foragers came together as agricultural communities. Do you think global climate change in the twenty-first century could alter the nature of the communities we live in? Will it, perhaps, lead to the creation of entirely new types of lifeways, which is what happened 11,000 years ago?

A carving of Kaban-Puuc, the ancient Maya god of maize (corn) and rain.

to find new land to farm. Although agriculture may have seemed an unattractive option to many foragers, farming communities usually had more resources and more people than foraging communities. When conflict occurred, more resources and more people usually meant that farming communities also had more power. Agriculture spread most easily in regions that bordered established agricultural zones and that had similar soils, climates, and ecologies. Where environmental conditions were different, the spread of agriculture had to await new techniques such as irrigation or new crops better adapted to the regions of new settlement.

Such changes are apparent, for example, as agriculture spread from southwestern Asia into the cooler and usually wetter environments of eastern, central, and northern Europe, or as maize cultivation spread northward from Mesoamerica, a process that depended in part on subtle genetic changes in local varieties of maize. Where new techniques were not available, foragers survived much longer, and the spread of agriculture could be checked, sometimes for thousands of years, as it was at the edge of the Eurasian steppes, which were not brought into cultivation until modern times. Usually agriculture spread through a process of budding off as villages became overpopulated and young families cleared and settled suitable land beyond the borders of their home villages.

General Characteristics and Long Trends

Agricultural communities share important characteristics that give the agrarian era an underlying coherence despite its extraordinary cultural diversity. These characteristics include societies based on villages, demographic dynamism, accelerated technological innovation, the presence of epidemic disease, new forms of power and hierarchy, and enduring relations with nonagrarian peoples.

VILLAGE-BASED SOCIETIES

At the base of all agrarian societies were villages, more or less stable communities of farming households. Although the crops, the technologies, and the rituals of villagers varied greatly from region to region, all such peasant communities were affected by the annual rhythms of harvesting and sowing, the demands of storage, the need for cooperation within and among households, and the need to manage relations with outside communities.

DEMOGRAPHIC DYNAMISM

The increased productivity of agriculture ensured that populations grew much faster than they had during the era of foragers. Rapid population growth ensured that villages and the technologies that sustained them would eventually spread to all regions in which agriculture was viable. Modern estimates suggest that during the agrarian era world population rose from 6 million ten thousand years ago to 770 million in 1750, at the beginning of the modern era. Although these figures hide enormous regional and chronological differences, they are equivalent to an average growth rate of approximately 0.05 percent per annum; on average, populations were doubling every fourteen hundred years. This rate can be compared with doubling times of eight thousand to nine thousand years during the era of foragers and approximately eighty-five years during the modern era.

ACCELERATED TECHNOLOGICAL INNOVATION

Local population pressure, expansion into new environments, and increasing exchanges of ideas and goods encouraged many subtle improvements in agricultural techniques. Most improvements arose from small changes in the handling of particular crops, such as earlier or later planting or the selection of better strains. However, on a broader scale, increased productivity arose from whole clusters of innovation that appeared in many environments. Swidden agriculturalists cleared forest lands by fire and sowed crops in the ashy clearings left behind; after a few years, when the soil's fertility was exhausted, they moved on. In mountainous areas farmers learned how to cultivate hillsides by cutting steplike terraces.

Secondary-Products Revolution
One of the most important of these clusters of innovation had its primary impact only in the Afro-Eurasian world zone. The archaeologist Andrew Sherratt called these changes the "secondary-products revolution." From about 4000 BCE a series of innovations allowed farmers in Afro-Eurasia to make more efficient use of the secondary products of large livestock—those products that could be exploited without slaughtering the animals. Secondary products include fibers, milk, manure for fertilizer, and traction power to pull plows, carry people, and transport goods. In arid regions, such as the steppes of Eurasia, the deserts of southwestern Asia, or the savanna lands of east Africa, the secondary-products revolution generated the entirely new lifeway of pastoralism as entire communities learned to live off the products of their herds. Unlike members of the farming communities that were most typical of the agrarian era, pastoralists were usually nomadic because in the dry grasslands in which pastoralism flourished livestock had to be moved constantly between pasturelands to provide them with enough feed.

The main impact of the secondary- products revolution was in farming areas, however, where horses, camels, and oxen began to be used to pull heavy plows and to transport goods and humans. The domestication of llamas meant that South America had some experience of the secondary-products revolution, but its major impact was felt in the Afro-Eurasian world zone because most potential domesticates had been driven to extinction in the Americas during the era of foragers. Many of the critical differences between the histories of Afro-Eurasia and the Americas may depend, ultimately, on this key technological difference.

Just Add Water
The techniques of water management known collectively as "irrigation" had an even greater impact on agricultural productivity. Irrigation farmers diverted small streams onto their fields, created new farm land by filling

The "Secondary-products" Revolution

As illustrated by the excerpt below from the University of Oxford website, the "secondary-productions" revolution is a theory that continues to be tested on artifacts dating back more than 6,000 years.

The first [project] involves the participation of Professor Andrew Sherratt, of the School of Archaeology of the University of Oxford and curator of the European prehistoric collections in the Ashmolean Museum. It was he who suggested that the first domestic animals may have been used not for their "secondary products" (milk, wool, hair and traction), but for meat, and that milking and the exploitation of other secondary animal products become part of prehistoric farming practices only around 4000 BCE. This socio-economic transition helped promote social evolutionary changes such as the birth of pastoral nomadic communities, the emergence of the Mediterranean farming economy and the rise of complex State-level societies.

The Oxford Levantine Archaeology laboratory has provided pottery sherds from vessels found in Israel's Negev desert dating from c. 4500–4000 BCE to test Sherratt's "secondary-products-revolution" hypothesis by analysing residues for evidence of milk. The samples are currently being tested in Professor Richard Evershed's Biogeochemistry Research Centre at the University of Bristol.

Source: Oxford Centre for Hebrew and Jewish Studies. (2004). Retrieved May 18, 2007, from http://www.ochjs.ac.uk/levantine.html

swamps with soil and refuse, or built systematic networks of canals and dams to serve entire regions. People practiced irrigation of some kind in Afro-Eurasia, in the Americas, and even in Papua New Guinea and the Pacific. Its impact was greatest in arid regions with fertile soils, such as the alluvial basins (regions whose soils were deposited by running water) of Egypt, Mesopotamia, the north of the Indian subcontinent, northern China, and the lowlands of the Andean region. In these regions irrigation agriculture was highly productive and led to exceptionally rapid population growth.

As agriculture spread and became more productive, it supported larger, denser, and more interconnected communities. Within these communities population pressure and increasing exchanges of information generated a steady trickle of innovations in building, warfare, record keeping, transportation and commerce, and science and the arts. These innovations stimulated further demographic growth in a powerful feedback cycle that explains why change was so much more rapid during the agrarian era than during the era of foragers. Yet innovation was rarely fast enough to keep up with population growth. This lag explains why, on the scale of decades or even centuries, all agrarian societies experienced cycles of expansion and collapse that obscured the underlying trend toward growth. These cycles underlay the more visible patterns of political rise and fall, commercial boom and bust, and cultural efflorescence (blooming) and decay that have so fascinated historians. (Such patterns of growth and decline can be described as "Malthusian cycles," after Thomas Malthus, the nineteenth-century English economist who argued that human populations will always rise faster than the supply of food, leading to periods of famine and sudden decline.)

EPIDEMIC DISEASES

Population growth could be slowed by epidemic diseases as well as by low productivity. Foraging communities were largely free of epidemic diseases because they were small and mobile, but farming communities created more favorable environments for pathogens (causative agents of disease). Close contact with livestock allowed pathogens to move from animals to humans, accumulations of rubbish provided fertile breeding grounds for diseases and pests, and large communities provided the abundant reserves of potential victims that epidemic diseases need to flourish and spread. Thus, as populations grew and exchanges between communities multiplied, diseases traveled more freely from region to region. Just as people had begun to hitch rides on domesticated animals, diseases began to hitch rides on people. The impact of diseases took the form of a series of epidemiological decrescendos that began with catastrophic epidemics, followed by less disastrous outbreaks as immune systems in region after region adapted to the new diseases.

As the historian William McNeill has shown, long-range epidemiological exchanges within the Afro-Eurasian world zone immunized the populations of this zone against a wide range of diseases to which populations in other world zones remained more vulnerable. Trans-Eurasian exchanges of diseases may help explain the slow growth of much of Eurasia during the first millennium CE because they caused deadly epidemics. But they may also explain why, once the world was united after 1492 CE, exchanges of diseases had a catastrophic impact on regions outside Afro-Eurasia. After all, people from Afro-Eurasia had acquired immunities to a much greater variety of diseases than people from less populous world zones.

HIERARCHIES OF POWER

In many tropical regions people harvested root crops piecemeal as the crops were needed. In regions of grain farming, however, such as southwestern Asia, China, and Mesoamerica, plants ripened at the same time; thus, entire crops had to be harvested and stored in a short period. For this reason grain agriculture required people, for the first time in history, to accumulate and store large surpluses of food. As villages of grain farmers multiplied and their productivity rose, the size of stored surpluses grew. Conflicts over control of these increasingly valuable surpluses often triggered the emergence of new forms of inequality and new systems of power.

Stored surpluses allowed communities for the first time to support large numbers of nonfarmers: specialists such as priests, potters, builders, soldiers, or artists who did not farm but rather supported themselves by exchanging their products or services for foodstuffs and other goods. As farmers and nonfarmers exchanged goods and services, a complex division of labor appeared for the first time in human history. Specialization increased interdependence between households and communities and tightened the webs of obligation and dependence that bound individuals and communities together.

Thought Experiment

Vocational tests help narrow down a multitude of career possibilities to some specific fields that match a person's personality and interests. That's especially valuable for students and important for the greater good. Consider how well modern society would work if everyone had the same job. Then imagine what that job would probably be. (Ask a farmer!)

Eventually surpluses grew large enough to support elite groups whose lives depended primarily on their ability to control and manage the resources produced by others, either through exchanges of goods and services or through the threat of force. Human societies became multilayered as some groups began to specialize in the exploitation of other men and women, who exploited farmers, who exploited the natural environment. William McNeill has called these elite groups "macroparasites," whereas the anthropologist Eric Wolf has called them "tribute takers."

RELATIONS WITH NONAGRARIAN COMMUNITIES

Finally, the agrarian era was characterized by complex relations between agrarian communities and other types of communities. Throughout this era pastoralists and foragers living outside the main agricultural regions continued to have a significant impact on agrarian communities by carrying goods between agrarian regions and sometimes by introducing technologies (such as the many technologies associated with pastoralism, from improved saddles to improved weaponry) or by trading valued goods such as furs or ivory or feathers.

Agrarian Communities Before Cities: 8000–3000 BCE

The *early* agrarian era is that time when agrarian communities existed, but no large cities or states. In Afro-Eurasia this time extended from about 8000 BCE until about 3000 BCE, when the first cities emerged; in the Americas this time began later and lasted longer, and in parts of the Australasian and Pacific world zones it lasted until modern times.

A WORLD OF VILLAGES

During the early agrarian era villages were the largest communities on Earth and the most important sources of demographic and technological dynamism. In today's world, in which villages are marginal demographically, technically, culturally, and politically, we could all too easily forget the crucial historical role that villages played for many millennia. During the early agrarian era most villages practiced forms of agriculture that anthropologists might refer to as "horticulture" because they depended mainly on the labor of humans (and particularly of women, if modern analogies can be relied on), whereas their main agricultural implements were digging sticks of many kinds. However, these communities also pioneered important innovations such as irrigation and terracing, which eventually allowed the appearance of more populous communities. Thus, villages accounted for much of the demographic and geographical expansion of the agrarian world through many thousands of years.

EMERGENCE OF HIERARCHY

Within the villages of the early agrarian era men and women began to encounter new problems caused by the fact that so many people were living together in relatively small spaces. As communities became larger, people had to find new ways of defining their relationships with neighbors, determining who had access to stored resources, administering justice, and organizing warfare, trade, and religious worship. As specialization spread, communities had to find ways of regulating exchanges and conflicts between persons whose interests and needs were increasingly diverse. The simple kinship rules that had provided all the regulation necessary in small foraging communities now had to be supplemented with more elaborate rules regulating behavior between people whose contacts were more anonymous, more fleeting, and less personal. Projects involving entire communities, such as building temples, building canals, and waging warfare, also required new types of leadership.

The archaeological evidence shows how these pressures, all linked to the growing size and density of human communities, led to the creation of institutionalized political and economic hierarchies, with wealthy rulers, priests, and merchants at one pole and property-less slaves or vagrants at the other pole. Archaeologists suspect the presence of institutionalized hierarchies wherever burials or residences begin to vary greatly in size within a community. Where children were buried with exceptional extravagance, we can be pretty sure that emerging hierarchies were hereditary, so parents could pass their status on to their children. Where monumental structures appeared, such as the statues on Easter Island in the Pacific Ocean, or giant stone circles such as Stonehenge in Britain, we can be certain that leaders existed with enough power to organize and coordinate the labor of hundreds or thousands of persons.

EARLY GLASS CEILING

Gender hierarchies may have been among the earliest institutionalized hierarchies. As members of households established more complex relationships with outsiders, they came under the influence of new rules, structures, and

Terracing

Terraced fields snaking up hillsides are spectacular sights and major tourist attractions in Southeast Asian nations such as the Philippines and Indonesia. Some of the terraces have been maintained for over 2000 years. The following extract describing the types of terraces built by the Ifugao ethnic group of the northern Philippines indicates that terracing is more complex than it appears from a distance.

Habal "swidden" (slope field, camote field, kaingin). Slopeland, cultivated and often contour-ridged (and especially for sweet potatoes). Other highland dry-field crops (including taro, yams, manioc, corn, millet, mongo beans, and pigeon peas, but excluding rice except at elevations below 600–700 meters [2,000 feet] above sea level) are also cultivated in small stands or in moderately intercropped swiddens. Boundaries remain discrete during a normal cultivation cycle of several years.

Lattan "house terrace" (settlement, hamlet terrace, residential site). Leveled terrace land, the surface of which is packed smooth or paved but not tilled; serving primarily as house and granary yards, work space for grain drying, and so forth; discrete, often fenced or walled, and named...

Qilid "drained field" (drained terrace, ridged terrace). Leveled terrace land, the surface of which is tilled and ditch mounded (usually in cross-contour fashion) for cultivation and drainage of dry crops, such as sweet potatoes and legumes. Drained fields, though privately owned, are kept in this temporary state for only a minimum number of annual cycles before shifting (back) to a more permanent form of terrace use...

Payo "pond field" (bunded terrace, rice terrace, rice field). Leveled farmland, bunded [with embankments] to retain irrigation water for shallow inundation of artificial soil, and carefully worked for the cultivation of wet-field rice, taro, and other crops; privately owned discrete units with permanent stone markers; the most valued of all land forms.

Source: Conklin, H. C. (1967–68). Some aspects of ethnographic research in Ifugao. *New York Academy of Sciences, Transactions,* ser. 2, 30, 107–108.

expectations. An emerging division of labor also created new opportunities outside the household and the village. Yet, in a world where the economic and social success of every farming household depended on bearing and rearing as many children as possible, women usually had fewer opportunities to take on more specialized roles—some of which brought great wealth and power. The linguist and archaeologist Elizabeth Barber has argued that this fact may explain why men were more likely to occupy high-ranking positions in emerging hierarchies. Warfare may also have changed gender relations as population growth intensified competition between communities and as men began to monopolize the organization of violence.

Whatever the cause, the disproportionate presence of men in power structures outside the village reshaped relations and attitudes within the village and the household. Men began to claim a natural superiority based on their role in emerging power structures outside the household, and women were increasingly defined by their role within the household and their relationships to men. Even the many women who earned money outside the household usually did so in jobs associated with the tasks of the household. Within the household the demands of peasant life ensured that men and women continued to work in partnership. At this intimate, domestic scale relationships owed as much to personal qualities as to gender. However, beyond the household the powerful web of cultural expectations and power relations now known as "patriarchy" emerged.

Worth Debating

If your school was buried in a volcano today and dug up a thousand years from now, what clues would help archaeologists figure out who were the leaders of the school? If the size of the room meant something to the investigators of the future, perhaps the Phys Ed teacher (leading activities in the gym) would seem to be the person with the most authority. If books counted, maybe the school librarian would appear to hold the power position. If the archeologists of the future knew what checks or credit cards looked like, they might focus, instead, on the business office.

LEADERS AND LEADERSHIP

Hierarchies of power shaped many other relationships as local communities were drawn into wider networks of exchange. In these larger networks traditional kinship thinking no longer worked. Genealogies began to take on semifictional forms that allowed entire communities to claim descent from the same, often mythical ancestor. Such genealogies could generate new forms of hierarchy by ranking descent groups according to their exact relationship to the founder. Where descendants of senior lines claimed higher status, aristocracies began to appear. When people chose leaders, however, ability often counted for as much as birth. Where high-born people lacked leadership skills, persons with more talent as conciliators, warriors, or mediators with the gods were often chosen to support or replace them. Most simple forms of leadership derived from the needs of the community; thus, they depended largely on popular consent. This consent made early power structures fragile because the power of leaders could evaporate all too easily if they failed in the tasks for which they were chosen.

As communities expanded, however, the resources available to their leaders increased until leaders began to set aside a share of those resources to support specialist enforcers or rudimentary armies. In this way leaders whose power originated in the needs of their subjects eventually acquired the ability to coerce at least some of those they ruled and to back up the collection of resources and the control of labor with the threat of force. The details of such processes are largely hidden from us, although archaeological evidence and anthropological research can give us many hints of how some of these processes played out in particular communities. These processes prepared the way for the more powerful political structures that we know as "states." States appeared in parallel with the large, sedentary communities we know as "cities."

The Earliest Cities and
States: 3000–500 BCE

For those people who define history as "the study of the past through written records," the period from 3000 BCE to 500 BCE was when history truly began because this was when the first written documents appeared in the two largest world zones: Afro-Eurasia and the Americas. Everything we have discussed so far would count, merely as "prehistory." From the perspective of world history this period marked a new stage in the complexity and size of human communities. In Afro-Eurasia, the largest and most populous of all world zones, the first cities and states appeared about 3000 BCE. In the Americas they appeared more than two thousand years later, in Mesoamerica and Peru. In the Australasian zone neither cities nor states appeared during the agrarian era; but in the Pacific zone embryonic states emerged on islands such as Tonga or Hawaii within the last thousand years.

If a single process accounts for the emergence of the first cities and states, it is increasing population density. The earliest cities and states appeared where people were most closely packed together, often because of the rapid expansion of irrigation agriculture. Sudden increases in population density intensified all the problems of coordination and control posed by large communities and greatly increased the need for specialist leaders. Rapid growth also multiplied the resources available to leaders. This is why the earliest cities appeared at about the same time as the earliest states. Cities can be defined as "large communities with a complex internal division of labor." (In contrast, villages, and even some early towns, such as the town of Catalhoyuk in Turkey, which dates from 6000 BCE, normally consisted of roughly similar households, mostly engaged in agriculture, with limited hierarchies of wealth and little specialization of labor.) States can be defined as "power structures that rest on systematic and institutionalized coercion as well as on popular consent."

Cities and states appeared as part of a cluster of social innovations, all of which were linked to the increasing scale and complexity of human societies in regions of highly productive agriculture. These innovations included the organization of specialized groups of officials and soldiers, writing, coercive forms of taxation, and monumental architecture.

AFRO–EURASIA AND THE AMERICAS

Because such an intimate connection existed between agricultural intensification and the appearance of cities and states, we should not be surprised that the earliest evidence for cities and states comes from regions with ancient agricultural traditions. The earliest clear evidence for communities large enough to be called "cities" and powerful enough to be called "states" comes from the ancient corridor from the Nile Valley to Mesopotamia that links Africa and Eurasia. Some of the earliest states appeared during the centuries before 3000 BCE in southern Mesopotamia in the region known

Documenting a Neolithic Settlement in the Electronic Age

Since 1993, an international team of archaeologists has been excavating the ancient city of Catalhoyuk in present-day Turkey, resuming an effort first begun in the 1960s. In an effort to bring alive the 9,000-year-old artifacts being found at the Catalhoyuk "dig," team member Rebecca Daly maintains a blog on the excavation website. Below is her entry for 28 July 2004.

Bleda is beginning the burial that was next to the sheep today, which thrills both of us, because we both suspect that there is some incredible stuff in that burial. There are a lot of burials coming out now, the human remains lab are tearing their hair out trying to get everything done. Just when they think they're going to catch up, more things appear! Sure enough, Bleda has come up with an interesting bird bone thing that both he and Lori, who's from the human remains lab doing the burial, think is a flute. It's certainly the right shape, and it has had both of the ends knocked off which suggests they wanted to use the inside for something. I have high hopes, Bleda seems to attract the interesting objects. It would be really amazing if this is actually a flute of some sort, it would be the earliest musical instrument. The burial was sprinkled with ochre both under and over it, which suggests that it was a really important part of the burial process in this case. This was obviously a very significant burial anyway, what with the whole lamb, but this makes it even more so—there is some suggestion of the order in which the burial activities took place.

Source: Mysteries of Catalhoyuk. (2004). Retrieved April 8, 2007, from http://www.catalhoyuk.com/history.html

to archaeologists as "Sumer" and also along the Nile River in modern Egypt and Sudan. During the next thousand years evidence of cities and states appeared also in the Indus River valley in modern Pakistan and in northern China.

In the Americas we can trace a similar pattern of evolution from villages toward cities and states, but the earliest evidence for both changes came much later. Although large communities and powerful leaders existed in Mesoamerica in the lands of the Olmecs (in Mexico's southern Gulf coast) by the second millennium BCE, most archaeologists would argue that the first true cities and states in the Americas appeared late during the first millennium BCE, in regions such as the Oaxaca Valley or farther south in the heartland of Mayan civilization. In the Andes, too, statelike communities, such as the Moche culture, appeared at the end of the first millennium BCE.

AGRARIAN CIVILIZATIONS

From these and other core areas the traditions of early statehood spread to nearby regions as populations expanded and networks of material and cultural exchanges knit larger regions together, generating greater concentrations of wealth and power. As they spread, states carried with them a core set of institutions and practices associated with what are often called "agrarian civilizations." Directly or indirectly, the spread of agrarian civilizations reflected the increasing scale and density of human populations. Cities were simply the most concentrated and largest of all human communities. States were the large, coercive power structures that were necessary to administer and defend city-scale communities, and they were supported economically by the large concentrations of wealth found in cities and their hinterlands.

Collecting that wealth by force often began with crude forms of looting that eventually turned into the more formalized looting that we call "taxation." Managing large stores of wealth required new forms of administration and new forms of accounting; indeed, in all emerging states writing apparently emerged first as a technique to keep track of large stores of wealth and resources. Even in the Inca state, where no fully developed system of writing emerged, rulers used a system of accounting based on intricately knotted strings (quipu).

Defending large concentrations of wealth and maintaining order within and between cities and city-states (autonomous states consisting of a city and surrounding territory) required the creation of armies. In Sumer and elsewhere invading armies possibly established the first states, and certainly all early states engaged enthusiastically in warfare. The rulers of the earliest states also engaged in symbolic activities that were equally vital to the maintenance of their power. They organized extravagant displays of wealth, often involving human sacrifices, and built palaces, temples, and monuments to the dead, often in the form of pyramids or ziggurats (temple towers consisting of a lofty pyramidal structure built in successive stages with outside staircases and a shrine at the top). These elaborate structures were designed to raise the prestige of local rulers and of the cities they ruled and the gods they worshiped.

IMPERIAL STATES

Through time the scale of state systems expanded as city-states traded with and sometimes absorbed other city-states. Eventually imperial systems emerged in which a single ruler controlled a large region of many cities and towns. Sargon of Akkad (reigned c. 2334 BCE–2279 BCE) may have established the first imperial state, in Mesopotamia, north of Sumer. By the middle of the second millennium BCE the Shang dynasty (approximately 1766–1045 BCE) had created an imperial state in northern China. Through time such states became more common. As states expanded, they taxed and administered larger areas, either directly or indirectly through local rulers. Improvements in transportation and communications, such as the appearance of wheeled vehicles in Afro-Eurasia during the second millennium BCE, extended the reach of states, their officials, and their armies.

Their influence reached much further than their power, however, as traders bridged the gaps between states, creating large networks of commercial and cultural exchange. Indeed, some experts have claimed that as early as 2000 BCE exchanges along the Silk Roads connecting China and the Mediterranean had already created a single, Eurasia-wide system of exchanges.

As impressive as these large and powerful communities were, we should remember the limits of their power and influence. Few agrarian states took much interest in the lives of their citizens as long as they paid their taxes and supplied their labor power when it was needed. Maintaining law and order outside of the major cities was usually left to regional rulers or nobles. Vast territories also lay beyond the direct control of imperial rulers. The scholar Rein Taagepera has estimated that early during the

Thought Experiment

In the twenty-first century, extravagant displays of wealth—palatial estates, jewels, and the like—remain a means to show great affluence. How do you think wealth will be shown a century from now? Is it possible that extravagant displays of wealth would be frowned on? Or maybe we'd start giving things away to show our wealth, as the Native Americans did in their potlatch ceremonies. After all, Bill Gates is busy giving away his billions. (Well, a lot of them!)

first millennium BCE states still controlled no more than about 2 percent of the area controlled by states today. Beyond this tiny area, which probably included most of the world's population, smaller communities of foragers, independent farmers, and pastoralists existed.

Although agrarian civilizations usually regarded these outside communities as barbarians, they could play a crucial role in providing sources of innovation and in linking agrarian civilizations. For example, steppe pastoralists in Eurasia transported religious ideas, metallurgical traditions, and even goods between China, India, and the Mediterranean world, and they may also have pioneered some of the military and transportation technologies of agrarian civilizations, such as the wheeled chariot. The most innovative naval technologies of this period were found in the western Pacific, where peoples of the Lapita culture, using huge double-hulled canoes, settled a vast area from New Guinea to Fiji and Tonga between 3000 and 1000 BCE.

Long-term growth in the number, size, and power of cities and states reflected not only innovations in statecraft and warfare, but also the sustained demographic buoyancy of the entire agrarian era. Our figures are too vague to allow much precision, but clearly, at least in the long trend, populations grew faster in areas of agriculture than elsewhere. They probably did not grow much faster than during the early agrarian era, however. Particularly in the cities, with their appalling sanitary conditions, bad air, and filthy water, death rates were extraordinarily high. Although cities offered more opportunities, they also killed people far more effectively than the villages. Population growth was also slowed by periodic demographic collapses. The spread of diseases into regions whose populations lacked immunities may have caused some of these collapses; overexploitation of the land, which could undermine the productive basis of entire civilizations, may have caused others. In southern Mesopotamia toward the end of the third millennium BCE, populations fell sharply, probably as a result of over-irrigation, which created soils too salty to be farmed productively. Archaeologists can trace the progress of salinization during the late second millennium through the increasing use of barley, a more salt-tolerant grain than wheat.

Agriculture, Cities, and Empires: 500 BCE–1000 CE

Most of the long trends that began after 3000 BCE continued during the period from 500 BCE to 1000 CE. Global populations rose (although they did so slowly during the middle of this period), the power, size, and number of states increased, and so did the extent of exchange networks. As agriculture spread, cities and states appeared in once-peripheral regions in northwestern Europe, sub-Saharan Africa, southern India, and southern China. Increasingly, agrarian civilizations encroached on regions inhabited by foragers, independent peasants, and pastoralists. Similar processes occurred in the Americas but with a time lag of approximately two thousand years.

AFRO–EURASIA

The Achaemenid empire, created in Persia (modern Iran) during the sixth century BCE, marked a significant increase in state power because the empire controlled a region five times as large as the greatest of its predecessors. During the next fifteen hundred years empires on this scale became the norm. They included the Han dynasty in China (206 BCE–220 CE), the Roman empire in the Mediterranean (27 BCE–476 CE), and the Mauryan empire (c. 324–c. 200 BCE) in India. The Muslim Abbasid empire, which ruled much of Persia and Mesopotamia from 749/750 CE (eventually collapsing only in 1258), controlled a slightly larger area than its Achaemenid predecessors. Contacts also flourished between imperial states. During the sixth century BCE Cyrus I, the founder of the Achaemenid empire, invaded parts of modern central Asia. When the Chinese emperor, Han Wudi, invaded the same region three centuries later, the separate agrarian civilizations of the Mediterranean world and eastern Asia came into closer

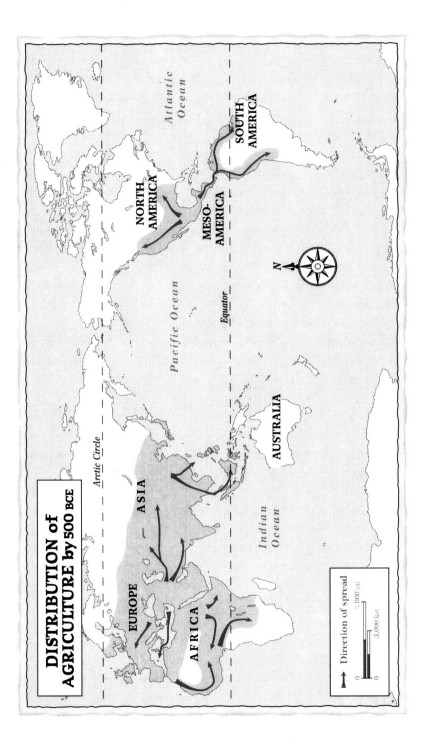

DISTRIBUTION of
AGRICULTURE by 500 BCE

Direction of spread

contact than ever before, binding the whole of Eurasia into the largest system of exchange on Earth.

The increased reach of political, commercial, and intellectual exchange networks may explain another important development during this era: the emergence of religious traditions that also extended over huge areas—the first world religions. Whereas earlier religious traditions usually claimed the allegiance of particular communities or regions, world religions claimed to express universal truths and to represent universal gods—reflections, perhaps, of the increasing scale of imperial states, and their need to reconcile the beliefs of diverse populations over very large areas.

The first world religion was probably Zoroastrianism, a religion whose founder may have come from central Asia during the sixth century BCE, at about the time when Cyrus I founded the Achaemenid empire. Buddhism was founded soon after in northern India during a period of rapid urbanization and state expansion. Its great period of expansion came early during the first millennium CE, when it began to spread in central Asia, China, and southeastern Asia. The influence of Christianity

Topics for Further Study

Buddhism

Catholicism, Roman

Christianity

Confucianism

Hinduism

Islam

Judaism

Manichaeism

Zoroastrianism

expanded within the Roman empire until, during the fourth century CE, it became the official religion of the state, under the emperor Constantine.

Both Buddhism and Christianity spread into central Asia and eventually reached China, although of the two only Buddhism made a significant impact on Chinese civilization. Even more successful was Islam, founded in southwestern Asia during the seventh century. Islam spread into north Africa, central Asia, India, and southeastern Asia, carried first by armies of conquest and later by the Muslim missionaries and holy men known as "sufis."

The same forces that gave rise to the first world religions may also have spurred some of the first attempts at universal generalizations about reality in early forms of philosophy and science. Although normally associated with the philosophical and scientific traditions of classical Greece, such ideas can also be found within the astronomical and mathematical

Worth Debating

Christianity, Buddhism, and Islam remain the most significant religions of the world. Until recent years, though, only Christianity has been a major presence in the United States. Do you see a greater presence of adherents of Buddhism and Islam in your own community? If not, search online for the words "Buddhist temple" or "mosque" and add in the name of the town or city you live in—you might be surprised at the results. Many ethnic groups have found their way into the American mainstream, but most of these groups observed religions rooted in Judeo-Christian theology and traditions. Will it take many years for other religions like Buddhism and Islam to find mainstream acceptance in the United States of the twenty-first century?

traditions of Mesopotamia and the philosophical traditions of northern India and China.

THE AMERICAS

In the Americas, too, political systems expanded in size, in military power, and in cultural and commercial reach. During the first millennium CE complex systems of city-states and early empires emerged in Mesoamerica. At its height the great city of Teotihuacan in Mexico had a population of more than 100,000 people and controlled trade networks reaching across much of Mesoamerica. We cannot be certain that it had direct control of any other cities or states, however. Farther south, Mayan civilization consisted of a large number of regional states, some of which may have established at least temporary control over their neighbors. Both these powerful systems collapsed, however, during the second half of the first millennium CE. As in southern Mesopotamia early during the second millennium BCE, the collapse may have been caused by overexploitation of the land.

However, just as the political traditions of Sumer were eventually taken up in Babylon and Assyria, so, too, in Mesoamerica the political traditions of Teotihuacan and the Maya provided the cultural foundations for even more powerful states during the next period of the agrarian era. In the Andes, too, cities and states began to appear; the first may have been the Moche state of northern Peru, which flourished for almost eight hundred years during the first millennium CE. Like Teotihuacan, the Moche kingdom influenced a large area, although we cannot be certain how much direct political power it had over other cities and states. During the later half of the first millennium statelike powers also emerged farther south in the lands near Lake Titicaca on the border between modern Peru and Bolivia.

EXPANSION IN OTHER AREAS

Populations also grew beyond the zone of agrarian civilization, generating new forms of hierarchy. In the thinly populated steppe zones of Eurasia, pastoral nomads began to form large, mobile confederations that raided and taxed neighboring agricultural zones. In Mongolia in central Asia the Xiongnu people created a spectacular empire during the second century BCE, as did the founders of the first Turkic empire during the sixth century CE. At its height the first Turkic empire reached from Mongolia to the Black Sea. In the Pacific zone migrants from the islands near Fiji began to settle the islands of Polynesia, scattered through the central and eastern Pacific. Hawaii and remote Easter Island may have been settled by 600 CE, but New Zealand seems to have been the last part of Polynesia to be settled, some time after 1000. Polynesia was settled by farming peoples, and in some regions, including Tonga and Hawaii, population growth created the preconditions for significant power hierarchies.

Topics for Further Study

Andean States

Assyrian Empire

Byzantine Empire

China

Greece, Ancient

Mesoamerica

Mississippian Culture

Persian Empire

Roman Empire

Steppe Confederations

Turkic Empire

Finally, significant changes occurred even in regions where agriculture had still made few inroads. In North America the slow northward spread of maize cultivation led to the establishment of numerous agricultural or semi-agricultural communities, such as those known as the "Anasazi" or "Ancient Pueblo People" (on the Colorado Plateau at the intersection of present-day Arizona, New Mexico, Colorado, and Utah). In the eastern

A sixteenth-century Native American agricultural village as depicted by early English settlers in Virginia.

parts of North America, too, farming communities emerged in regions such as the Ohio River valley, where they cultivated local plants such as sunflowers. Even in Australia foraging communities intensified production and settled in denser communities, particularly along the coasts.

Agricultural Societies on the Eve of the Modern Revolution: 1000–1750

During the last period of the agrarian era, from 1000 to 1750, earlier trends continued, but fundamental changes also hinted at the imminent changes of the modern era.

Agriculture spread into previously marginal regions such as North America, southern Africa, and western China. Often migrant farmers settled new lands with the active support of metropolitan merchants or governments. World populations continued to grow, despite sharp declines in much of Eurasia after the Black Death (bubonic plague) of the fourteenth century and in the Americas during the sixteenth century after the arrival of Afro-Eurasian diseases such as smallpox. The sixteenth-century economic and demographic collapse in the Americas was catastrophic; the population of indigenous Americans may have declined by anything from 50 percent to 90 percent in the century after Columbus. But it was offset in the long run by the arrival of immigrants, livestock, and new crops from Eurasia and the subsequent expansion of land under cultivation. In agriculture, weaponry, transportation (particularly seaborne transportation), and industry, a steady trickle of innovations sustained growth by gently raising average productivity and enhancing state power. The economist Angus Maddison has estimated that global gross domestic product (GDP, the total production of goods and services) rose from approximately $120 billion (in 1990 international dollars) in 1000 to almost $700 billion in 1820.

CREATION OF GLOBAL NETWORKS

The most important change during this era was the unification of the major world zones during the sixteenth century. This unification created the first global networks of exchanges. The linking of regions that had had no contact for many thousands of years generated a commercial and intellectual synergy that was to play a critical role in the emergence of the modern world.

In Afro-Eurasia the most striking feature of the early part of the last millennium was the increasing scale and intensity of international contacts. Viking raiders and traders traveled in central Asia, in the Mediterranean, along the coast of western Europe, even in distant Iceland and Greenland, and in 1000 they even created a short-lived colony in Newfoundland, Canada. The astonishing conquests of the Mongols early during the thirteenth century created a huge zone of relative

Topics for Further Study

Aztec Empire

European Expansion

Islamic World

Mongol Empire

Ottoman Empire

Trading Patterns, China Seas

Trading Patterns, Indian Ocean

Trading Patterns, Mediterranean

Trading Patterns, Pacific

Trading Patterns, Trans-Saharan

Viking Society

Thought Experiment

Although widespread diseases like bubonic plague and smallpox ravaged populations of the past, we are now living through the worst pandemic in human history. What disease is causing it? And have you noticed its presence? Between 1981 and 2001 alone, more people died from HIV/AIDS than from any other disease in human history. Despite worldwide economic, social, and medical programs to treat and control AIDS, the pandemic is far from over. What are the chances that AIDS will be conquered in your lifetime?

peace extending from Manchuria to the Mediterranean, and, with Mongol protection, the trade routes of the Silk Roads flourished during the late thirteenth and early fourteenth centuries. Sea routes were equally active, and exchanges of goods by sea from the Mediterranean through southern and southeastern Asia to China became routine. Briefly during the early fifteenth century huge Chinese fleets dispatched by Ming emperors and commanded by a Muslim admiral, Cheng Ho, made a series of expeditions to the West, some of which took them to Arabia in southwestern Asia and to east Africa.

Control of the Eurasian heartlands of Persia and central Asia—first by the Muslim empire of the Abbasids late during the first millennium and then by the Mongols—encouraged the exchange of technologies, goods, and religious and cultural traditions throughout Eurasia. In the Americas the first imperial states appeared. The most successful and best known were those of the Aztecs, based at Tenochtitlan in Mexico, and of the Incas, based at Cuzco in Peru. These were the first American polities (political organizations) to exert direct political and military control over very large areas.

However, the small, highly commercialized states of western Europe, not imperial states, eventually linked the separate world zones of the agrarian era by creating the first global networks of sea-borne transportation. The first significant states had emerged in western Europe during the first millennium CE as the region had been absorbed within the commercial and cultural hinterland of the Roman empire. During the ninth century Charlemagne and his successors tried to reestablish the Roman empire in western Europe. Their failure helps explain why Europe emerged as a region of highly competitive medium-sized states. Because such states had a more limited tax base than great imperial powers such as the Abbasid empire or China's Tang (618–907 CE) empire, they had to seek alternative sources of revenue, including revenues from trade, to survive the vicious warfare that became the norm in this region.

Not surprisingly, a tradition of predatory, militaristic trading states emerged. Blocked in the eastern Mediterranean, European powers sought new ways of cutting into the great markets of southern and eastern Asia, and this search, backed aggressively by European governments, eventually encouraged European merchants, led by the Portuguese, to circle the globe in their small but highly manoeuvrable and heavily armed ships. The wealth that European states secured as they cut in on the profits of the great trading systems of southeastern Asia and the even more spectacular gains they made by conquering the great civilizations of Central and South America repaid the initial investment of money and resources many times over.

IMPACT OF GLOBAL NETWORKS

The Americas and Europe were the first regions to be transformed by the new global system of exchanges. In eastern Eurasia the incursions of Europeans had a limited impact for a century or more. Portuguese and

A display of burial goods recovered from the burial mounds of Agrarian era farmers in southeastern Missouri.

Spanish ships, followed a century later by Dutch and English ships, seized important trading ports and began to cut in on local trade, particularly in spices. They had little impact on the major polities of the region, however. In the Americas European weaponry, the breakdown of traditional political and economic structures, and, perhaps most important of all, the impact of Eurasian pathogens such as smallpox crippled the Aztec and Inca empires and secured for the Spanish government an astonishing windfall of trade goods and precious metals that funded the first empire to straddle the Atlantic Ocean. As we have seen, European diseases were particularly destructive in the Americas because most natives lacked immunity to the diseases that had spread through Afro-Eurasia through many centuries.

Control of global trade networks brought European states great commercial wealth, but it also brought an influx of new information about geography, the natural world, and the customs of other societies. The torrent of new information available to European intellectuals may have played a critical role in undermining traditional certainties and creating the skeptical, experimental cast of mind that we associate with the so-called scientific revolution. Deprived of old certainties by a flood of new knowledge, European thinkers had to think everything over anew, and they had to experiment with new ideas.

No region on Earth was entirely unaffected by the creation of the first global system of exchanges, however. The exchange of goods between the Americas and Afro-Eurasia stimulated population growth throughout Afro-Eurasia as crops such as maize, cassava, and potatoes spread to China, Europe, and Africa, where they supplemented existing crops or allowed people to cultivate lands unsuitable for other crops. The abundant silver of the Americas gave a huge boost to international trade, particularly after Chinese governments began to demand the payment of taxes in silver from the 1570s, pulling more and more silver toward what was still the largest single economy in the world. New drugs such as tobacco and coca became available for the first time to Afro-Eurasian consumers, whereas older drugs, such as tea, circulated more widely, stimulating consumer demand in cities from Istanbul to Mexico City.

Perhaps most important of all, the position of Europe within global networks of exchange was transformed. As long as the world was divided into separate zones, Europe could be little more than a marginal borderland of Afro-Eurasia. The hub of Eurasian networks of exchange lay in the Islamic heartland of Persia and Mesopotamia. In the integrated world system that emerged during the sixteenth century, European states found themselves at the hub of the largest and most vigorous exchange networks that had ever existed. The huge flows of wealth and information that coursed through these networks would transform the role and significance of Europe and the Atlantic region in world history, and eventually they would transform the entire world.

Agrarian Era in World History

The introduction of agricultural technologies raised productivity, increased populations, and stimulated innovation. These developments explain why change was so much more rapid during the agrarian era than during the era of foragers. Larger, denser communities created new problems, which were solved by forming the large, hierarchical structures that we call "states," "empires," and "civilizations." Within these structures the very nature of human communities was transformed as families and households found themselves incorporated in, and disciplined by states, religions, and market forces. The exchange of technologies and goods between larger regions and larger populations stimulated many small improvements in agrarian techniques, communications technologies, and the technologies of information storage and warfare. However, although innovation was much faster than it had been during the era of foragers, it was rarely fast enough to keep pace with population growth, which is why, on the smaller scales that meant most to rulers and their subjects, the characteristic rhythm of change during the agrarian era was cyclical.

The modern world built on the slow accumulation of people, resources, and information that took place during the agrarian era, but it was marked out from this era by another sharp acceleration in rates of innovation that would lead to one more fundamental transformation in human lifeways.

Our World: The Modern Era

T he modern era is the briefest but most turbulent of the three main eras of human history. Whereas the era of foragers lasted more than 200,000 years and the agrarian era about 10,000 years, the modern era has lasted just 250 years. Yet during this brief era change has been more rapid and more fundamental than ever before; indeed, populations have grown so fast that 20 percent of all humans may have lived during just these two and a half centuries. The modern era is also the most interconnected of the three eras. Whereas new ideas and technologies once took thousands of years to circle the globe, today people from different continents can converse as easily as if they lived in a single global village. History has become world history in the most literal sense.

Here we make the slightly arbitrary assumption that the modern era began in about 1750. Yet its roots lay deep in the agrarian era, and we could make a good case for a starting date of 1500 or even earlier. Determining the end date of the modern era is even trickier. Some scholars have argued that it ended during the twentieth century and that we now live in a "postmodern" era that is radically different from the "modern" era. Yet many features of the modern era persist today and will persist for some time into the future; thus, it makes more sense to see our contemporary period as part of the modern era. This fact means that we do not know when the modern era will end, nor can we see its overall shape as clearly as we might wish.

The fact that we cannot see the modern era as a whole makes it difficult to specify its main features and justifies our use of the deliberately vague label, "modern." At present the diagnostic (defining) feature of the modern era seems to be a sharp increase in rates of innovation. New technologies enhanced human control over natural resources and stimulated rapid population growth. In their turn, technological and demographic

67

changes transformed lifeways, cultural and religious traditions, patterns of health and aging, and social and political relationships.

For world historians the modern era poses distinctive challenges. We are too close to see it clearly and objectively; we have so much information that we have difficulty distinguishing trends from details; and change has occurred faster than ever before and embraced all parts of the world. What follows is one attempt to construct a coherent overview based on generalizations that have achieved broad acceptance among world historians.

Major Features and Trends of the Modern Era

The modern era is the first to have generated a large body of statistical evidence; so it is also the first in which we can quantify many of the larger changes.

INCREASES IN POPULATION AND PRODUCTIVITY

Human populations have increased faster than ever before during the modern era, although growth rates slowed during the late twentieth century. Between 1750 and 2000 the number of human beings increased

❧ Key Features and Trends ❧ of the Modern Era

- Rapid Population Growth
- Technological Innovation
- Large Increase in Productivity
- Harnessing of Fossil and other Forms of Energy
- Large Communities
- Bureaucracy
- Nationalism
- Longer Life Expectancy
- Broader Role for Women
- Commercialization
- Global Networks
- Destruction of Foraging and Agrarian Lifeways

Worth Debating

How important will the attacks of September 11, 2001, appear in fifty years' time? Will they seem like a turning point in world history? As the beginning of a new round of global conflicts, perhaps? Or, more optimistically, is it possible that they will appear as a turning point in a world progressively freed of brutal world conflicts? What's your guess? And what's your hope?

from approximately 770 million to almost 6 billion, close to an eightfold increase in just 250 years. This increase is the equivalent of a growth rate of about 0.8 percent per annum and represents a doubling time of about eighty-five years. (Compare this with estimated doubling times of fourteen hundred years during the agrarian era and eight thousand to nine thousand years during the era of foragers.) An eightfold increase in human numbers was possible only because productivity increased even faster. The estimates of the economist Angus Maddison suggest that global gross domestic product rose more than ninetyfold between 1700 and 2000, and even production *per person* rose ninefold.

These astonishing increases in productivity lie behind all the most significant changes of the modern era. Productivity rose in part because new technologies were discovered and introduced. In agriculture, for example, food production has kept pace with population growth because of improved crop rotations, increased use of irrigation, widespread application of artificial fertilizers and pesticides, and the use of genetically modified crops. However, productivity also rose because humans learned to exploit new sources of energy. During the era of foragers, each human controlled, on average, a little more than 3,000 kilocalories a day, just enough to sustain a human body in a state of reasonable health. In the agrarian era each human controlled, on average, 12,000 kilocalories a day, and the most powerful prime movers available were domestic animals or wind-driven ships. During the modern era humans have learned to harvest the huge reserves of energy stored in fossil fuels such as coal, oil, and natural gas and even to exploit the power lurking within atomic nuclei. Today each person controls, on average, 230,000 kilocalories a day—twenty times as much as during the agrarian era. (That's the equivalent of eating almost 1,000 candy bars a day!) A world of planes, rockets, and nuclear power has replaced a world of horses, oxen, and wood fires.

CITY SPRAWL

As populations have increased, so has the average size of human communities. In 1500 about fifty cities had more than 100,000 inhabitants, and none had more than a million.

By 2000 several thousand cities had more than 100,000 inhabitants, about 411 had more than a million, and 41 had more than 5 million. (In 2007, the population of Shanghai, China, was estimated at almost 15.5 million.) During the agrarian era most people lived and worked in villages; by the end of the twentieth century almost 50 percent of the world's population lived in communities of at least five thousand people. The rapid decline of villages marked a fundamental transformation in the lives of most people on Earth. As during the agrarian era, the increasing size of

Top Ten Cities of the Year 1500

Below is the ranking and population of the most populous cities ranked back in 1500. The list of top ten cities some five hundred years later still includes two of these cities, though the population is vastly different—Beijing (8.7 million) and Istanbul (8.8 million).

1	Beijing, China	672,000
2	Vijayanagar, India	500,000
3	Cairo, Egypt	400,000
4	Hangzhou, China	250,000
5	Tabriz, Iran	250,000
6	Constantinople (Istanbul), Turkey	200,000
7	Gaur, India	200,000
8	Paris, France	185,000
9	Guangzhou, China	150,000
10	Nanjing, China	147,000

Source: Chandler, T. (1987). *Four thousand years of urban growth: An historical census by Tertius Chandler.* Lampeter, UK: St. David's University Press.

communities transformed lifeways, beginning with patterns of employment. Whereas most people during the agrarian world were small farmers, today most people support themselves by wage work in a huge variety of different occupations.

Innovations in transportation and communications have transformed relations between communities and regions. Before the nineteenth century no one traveled faster than the pace of a horse (or a fast sailing ship); when President Jefferson left office in 1809, he rode home to his Virginia estate of Monticello on horseback. The fastest way to transmit written messages was by state-sponsored courier systems that used relays of horses. Today messages can cross the world instantaneously, and even perishable goods can be transported from one end of the world to another in just a few hours or days.

INCREASINGLY COMPLEX AND POWERFUL GOVERNMENTS

As populations have grown and interconnections between people have multiplied, more complex forms of regulation have become necessary, which is why the business of government has been revolutionized. Most premodern governments were content to manage war and taxes, leaving their subjects to get on with their livelihoods more or less unhindered, but the managerial tasks facing modern states are much more complex, and they have to spend more effort in mobilizing and regulating the lives of those they rule. The huge bureaucracies of modern states are one of the most important by-products of the modern revolution. So, too, are the structures of democracy, which allow governments to align their policies more closely with the needs and capabilities of the large and varied populations they rule. Nationalism—the close emotional and intellectual identification of citizens with their governments—is another by-product of these new relationships between governments and those they rule.

The growth of democracy and nationalism may suggest that modern governments are more reluctant to impose their will by force, but in fact they have much more administrative and coercive power than did rulers of the agrarian era. No government of the agrarian era tried to track the births, deaths, and incomes of all the people it ruled or to impose compulsory schooling; yet many modern governments handle these colossal tasks routinely. Modern states can also inflict violence more effectively and on a larger scale than even the greatest empires of the agrarian era. Whereas an eighteenth-century cannon could destroy a house or kill a closely packed group of soldiers, modern nuclear weapons can destroy entire cities and millions of people, and the concerted launch of many nuclear weapons could end the story of human beings within just a few hours.

A subtler change in the nature of power is the increased dependence of modern states on commercial and economic success rather than raw coercion. Their power depends so much on the economic productivity of the societies they rule that modern governments have to be effective economic managers. The creation of more democratic systems of government, the declining importance of slavery, the ending of European imperial power during the twentieth century, the collapse of the Soviet command economy in 1991, and the ending of apartheid (racial segregation) in South Africa in 1990 and 1991 all reflected a growing awareness that skillful economic management raises productivity much more effectively than the cruder and more coercive forms of rule typical of the agrarian era.

GROWING GAP BETWEEN RICH AND POOR

Although wealth has accumulated faster than ever before, the gap between rich and poor has widened, both within and between countries. The estimates of Angus Maddison suggest that in 1820 the GDP per person of the United States was about three times that of all African states; by 1998 the ratio had increased to almost twenty times that of all African states. Yet some of the benefits of modern technologies have been shared more generally. Improvements in the production and supply of food and in sanitation, as well as improved understanding of diseases and the introduction of vaccinations (during the nineteenth century) and antibiotics (during the twentieth century) help explain why, for the first time in human history, so few people die in infancy or childhood that average life expectancies have more than doubled, rising from about twenty-six years in 1820 to about sixty-six years at the end of the twentieth century. These gains have not been shared equally, but all parts of the world have felt their impact.

IMPROVED OPPORTUNITIES FOR WOMEN

Relations between men and women have been renegotiated in many parts of the world. New energy sources have reduced the importance of physical strength in employment, new forms of contraception have given women and men more control over reproduction, and new technologies, such as bottle feeding, have allowed parents to share more easily in the task of caring for infants. Reduced infant mortality and new forms of socialized old-age support have reduced the pressure to have many children as a form of old-age insurance. Finally, urbanization and commercialization have created more varied forms of employment for women as well as men. Women are less closely tied to their traditional role as child rearers, particularly in the most industrialized regions of the world. Nevertheless, gender inequality still survives even in those societies most deeply transformed by the modern revolution. Even in the United States and western Europe the average wages of women lag behind those of men. According to the U.S. Department of Labor, "In 1992 for those receiving hourly rates, women's median hourly earnings were 79.4 percent of men's; for full-time wage and salary workers, women's median weekly earnings were 75.4 percent of men's; and median annual earnings for women were 70.6 percent of men's annual earnings in 1992, the most recent year for which data are available."

DESTRUCTION OF PREMODERN LIFEWAYS

Finally, the modern revolution has destroyed premodern lifeways. Until the twentieth century independent communities of foragers survived in many parts of the world, but by the end of the twentieth century no foragers lived outside a modern state, and their lifeways had been transformed as they had been forcibly brought into the modern world. Peasant farming—the lifeway of most women, men and children throughout the agrarian era—declined as peasant households were unable to compete with large, industrial agribusinesses or the commercial farmers of more industrialized countries. By the end of the twentieth century peasant farming had vanished in much of the world. Even where it survived—in much of east Asia and Africa, for example, as well as in much of Latin America—it was in decline. These changes marked the end of traditions, cultures, and lifeways that had shaped the lives of most humans throughout the earlier eras of human history.

Explaining the Modern Revolution

The key to these momentous changes was a sudden rise in the productivity of human labor caused by increasing rates of innovation. So, to explain modernity we must explain why rates of innovation have risen so fast

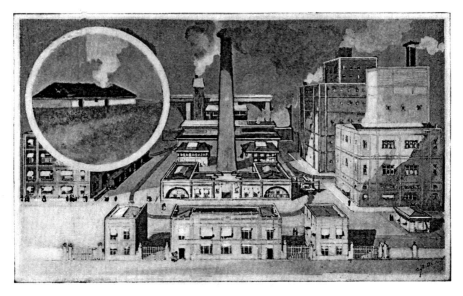

An early twentieth-century industrialized distilling plant. Note the contrast with the traditional Irish plant shown in the inset.

during the modern era. As yet no general agreement exists on the causes of the modern revolution or, indeed, on the general causes of innovation in human history. However, widespread agreement exists on some of the more important contributing factors.

ACCUMULATED CHANGES OF THE AGRARIAN ERA

First, the modern revolution clearly built on the accumulated changes of the agrarian era. Slow growth during several millennia had led to incremental technological improvements in agriculture and water management, in warfare, in mining, in metalwork, and in transportation and communications. Improvements in transportation and communications—such as the development of more maneuverable ships or the ability to print with movable type—were particularly important because they increased the scale of exchanges and ensured that new technologies, goods, and ideas circulated more freely. Methods of organizing large numbers of humans for warfare or tax collection also improved during the agrarian era. In ways that are not yet entirely clear, these slow technological and organizational changes, together with a steady expansion in the size and scale of global markets, created the springboard for the much faster changes of the modern era. During the final centuries of the agrarian era the pace of change was already increasing. International GDP grew almost sixfold between 1000 and 1820, whereas hardly any growth had occurred during the previous millennium.

RISE OF COMMERCIAL SOCIETIES

Second, most historians would agree that the modern revolution is connected with the rise of more commercial societies. From the Scottish economist Adam Smith onward economists have argued that a close link exists between innovation and commercial activity. Smith argued that large markets allow increased specialization, which encourages more precise and productive labor. Equally important, entrepreneurs buying and selling in competitive markets faced competition of a kind that landlords and governments of the agrarian era could usually avoid. To survive, entrepreneurs had to undercut their rivals by selling and producing goods at lower prices. To do that meant trading and producing with maximum efficiency, which usually meant finding and introducing the most up-to-date technology. As commercial exchanges spread, so did the number of wage workers: people who took their own labor to market. Because they competed with others to find work, wage workers also had to worry about the cheapness and productivity of their labor.

For these reasons the slow commercialization of societies that occurred throughout the agrarian era probably raised productivity by stimulating innovation. As the wealth, influence, and number of entrepreneurs and wage earners increased, the societies in which they lived became more open and receptive to innovation.

DEVELOPMENT OF A SINGLE GLOBAL NETWORK

Third, the linking of world zones into a single global network from the sixteenth century provided a sharp stimulus to commercial growth and technological innovation. In just a century or so the scale on which goods and ideas could be exchanged almost doubled, and a huge variety of new goods and ideas entered into global circulation. Maize, sugar, silver, coffee, cotton, tobacco, potatoes, and the productive and commercial expertise that went with these commodities were no longer confined to particular regions but instead were available throughout the world. Even the trade in people was internationalized. Before the sixteenth century the most active slave traders operated in the Islamic world, and most of their slaves came from Slavic or Turkic peoples to their north. From the sixteenth century European slavers began to capture or buy African slaves and to ship them to plantations in the Americas. For better or worse, such global exchanges stimulated commerce throughout the world.

WESTERN EUROPE'S EMERGENCE AS A GLOBAL HUB

Although change was rapid, it did not transform all parts of the world at once, and the order in which different regions were transformed had a profound effect on the course of modern history. This fact is the fourth factor contributing to the modern revolution. The societies of western Europe had been at the margins of the great trading systems of the agrarian era, but they were at the center of the global networks of exchange created during the sixteenth century because they controlled the oceangoing fleets that knit the world into a single system. Western Europe was better placed than any other region to profit from the vast flows of goods and ideas within the emerging global system of exchange. The European scientific revolution was, in part, a response to the torrent of new ideas pouring into Europe as a result of its expanded contacts with the rest of the world. Awareness

Thought Experiment

Different parts of the world often had different relative strengths and significance. Consider the world in 1789. China was probably the most populous, wealthiest, and most influential state on Earth; Europe was beginning to play a dominant role in the world's economy; much of North America was occupied by indigenous Americans or controlled by European colonial power; the United States was comparatively weak and insignificant economically. Now imagine a future world where China is once again the most populous, wealthiest, and most influential state on Earth, the European Union member nations form the world's largest economy, and the United States is much weaker and less significant economically. How would the United States—both the country and its citizenship—adapt to such a drop in prestige?

of new ideas, crops, religions, and commodities undermined traditional behaviors, cosmologies, and beliefs and posed sharply the question of how to distinguish between false and true knowledge of the world. The reinvention and spread of printing with movable type ensured that new information would circulate more easily in Europe than elsewhere.

At the same time European states, in an environment of almost continuous warfare, desperately needed new sources of revenue; thus, they were keen to exploit the commercial opportunities created within the global economic system. They did so partly by seizing the resources of the Americas and using American commodities such as silver to buy their way into the markets of southern and eastern Asia, the largest in the world. The increasing scale of commercial and intellectual exchanges within Europe created an environment that was particularly open to innovation because European innovators could draw on the intellectual and commercial resources of the entire world. The primacy of western Europe during the early stages of the modern revolution allowed it and the North American region to put their distinctive stamp on the modern era and to achieve a global hegemony that has so far lasted almost two centuries. Because of Europe's primacy English is the universal language of modern diplomacy and business, rather than Persian or Chinese, and suits and ties rather than kaftans are worn in the United Nations.

OTHER FACTORS

Fifth, more particular factors must enter into any detailed explanation of the modern revolution. The peculiarly commercialized nature of European states undoubtedly helps explain their receptiveness to innovation, but geographical factors, such as climatic changes, or the presence of large, relatively accessible seams of coal in Britain and northwestern Europe, may also have shaped the timing and geography of the modern revolution.

Industrial Revolution: 1750–1914

These arguments suggest that the ingredients of the modern revolution were present in all parts of the world, even though its full impact first became apparent in northwestern Europe and the eastern seaboard of what became the United States. In the Atlantic region technological change accelerated from the late eighteenth century. Familiar markers of change include the introduction and spread of more productive agricultural techniques, more efficient machines for spinning and processing cotton, the improved steam engine of the Scottish inventor James Watt, and the first locomotive. By the early nineteenth century contemporaries saw that something exceptional was happening. In 1837 the French revolutionary Auguste Blanqui (1805–1881) declared that an "industrial revolution" was underway in Britain and that it was as significant as the political revolutions that had re-

Topics for Further Study

Enlightenment

Industrialization

Urbanism

cently taken place in Europe and the Americas. By this time European levels of productivity had already overtaken those of the ancient superpowers of India and China.

THREE WAVES OF THE INDUSTRIAL REVOLUTION

The technological innovations of the Industrial Revolution spread in waves. Each wave spawned new productivity-raising technologies and spread industrialization to new regions. In the first wave, during the late eighteenth and early nineteenth centuries, the crucial changes occurred in Britain, although many of the innovations introduced there had been pioneered elsewhere. The most important changes were the introduction of efficient cotton-spinning machines and the Watt steam engine.

The steam engine provided for the first time an efficient way of exploiting the energy locked up in fossil fuels; it made available a seemingly endless supply of cheap energy, particularly in regions with ready access to coal. Immediately it lowered the cost of extracting coal by easing the task of pumping water from mine shafts. In combination with new spinning and weaving machines invented during the late eighteenth century, the steam engine also revolutionized the textile industry, the second-most-important sector (after agriculture) in most agrarian societies. To exploit these new technologies more efficiently, entrepreneurs began to bring workers together in the large, closely supervised productive workshops we know as factories.

In a second wave of innovations that occurred during the early and middle decades of the nineteenth century, steam engines were mounted on wheels to create the first locomotives. Railways slashed transportation costs over land, which is why they had a particularly revolutionary impact on the economies of large nations such as the United States and the Russian empire. In their turn, demand for coal, locomotives, rolling stock, and track stimulated coal and metal production and engineering. During the early nineteenth century many of these technologies spread to other parts of Europe and to the United States.

A third wave of innovations occurred during the second half of the nineteenth century. Industrial technologies spread in North America, in other parts of Europe, and in Russia and Japan. Military humiliation at the hands of Western nations during the 1850s and 1860s forced the governments of Russia and Japan to realize that they had to encourage industrialization if they were to survive, because industrial power clearly enhanced military power. Steel, chemicals, and electricity were the most important new technologies during this wave of the industrial revolution, and new forms of organization brought banks and factories together in large corporate enterprises, the largest of which were formed in the United States. In Germany and the United States systematic scientific research began to play an important role in technological innovation, as did large corporations, and innovation began to be institutionalized within the structures of modern business and government.

By the end of the nineteenth century Britain was losing its industrial primacy to Germany and the United States: in 1913 the United States accounted for almost 19 percent of the world's GDP, Germany for 9 percent, and the United Kingdom for just over 8 percent.

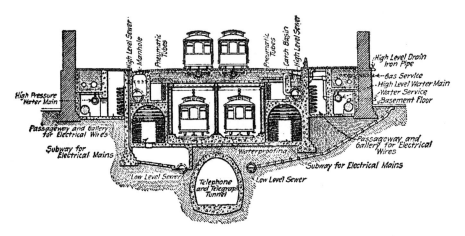

Subways have proven to be an efficient means of transportation in crowded cities. This diagram is a cross-section of the Chicago subway system in the early twentieth century.

ECONOMIC DEVELOPMENTS

The first three waves of industrialization transformed levels of productivity. Between 1820 and 1913 the GDP of the United Kingdom increased by more than six times, that of Germany by nine times, and that of the United States by forty-one times. During the same period GDP per capita increased by 2.9 times in the United Kingdom, by 3.4 times in the lands that became Germany, and by 4.2 times in the United States. No earlier era of human history had witnessed such astonishingly rapid increases in productivity.

Topics for Further Study

Colonialism

Imperialism

Liberalism

These growth rates were not matched in the rest of the world. On the contrary, the increasing economic and military might of the regions that industrialized first undermined the traditional agrarian societies of India, China, and the Ottoman empire. While the machine-produced textiles of the European and Atlantic powers undercut local products in other regions, their modernized armies conquered much of the world.

During the late nineteenth century interregional disparities in wealth and power increased sharply. Between 1820 and 1913 China's share of world GDP fell from 33 percent to 9 percent and that of India from 16 percent to 8 percent, while the share of the United Kingdom rose from 5 percent to more than 8 percent and that of the United States from almost 2 percent to more than 19 percent. By the end of the nineteenth century India was ruled by Britain; China was dominated commercially and even, to an extent, militarily by a conglomerate of European and Atlantic powers together with Japan; the Americas and Australasia were largely populated by migrants of European origin; much of Latin America was under the financial and commercial domination of Europe; and most of Africa and southeastern Asia had been incorporated within European empires. For the first time in human history political and economic inequalities between countries were becoming as striking as inequalities within countries. Global imperialism and the Third World are creations of the late nineteenth century.

DEMOCRATIC REVOLUTION

Economic changes were accompanied by profound social, political, and cultural changes. The peasant populations of agrarian societies were largely self-sufficient, but the urbanized wage-earning populations of industrialized societies, like the entrepreneurial classes that employed them, depended much more on structures of law and order and economic regulation that only states could provide. Governments, in turn, depended more on the cooperation of large sections of society as their tasks became more varied and complex. These changes explain the often violent renegotiation of relations between governments and subjects. The first modern democratic political systems emerged in the United States and western Europe during the turbulent second half of the eighteenth century, which the historian Robert Palmer called the "age of the democratic revolution." More democratic methods of rule granted political influence to wider sections of the population in exchange for increasing regulation, as governments, such as those of revolutionary France, began to recruit into mass armies, to take detailed censuses, and to regulate life in factories, offices, and even households.

CULTURAL CHANGES

Cultural life was transformed. Mass education spread literacy to a majority of the population in much of North America and Europe during the nineteenth century, while the emerging mass media gave citizens plenty to read and informed them of events in their own nation and the world at large. Mass education, combined with new forms of mass entertainment, also began to give citizens a more modern sense of a shared "national" identity. All religious traditions had to face the challenge posed by modern science, and most did so by incorporating some aspects of a new scientific view of reality while rejecting others. The spectacular successes of nineteenth-century science raised the prestige of science and challenged traditional worldviews.

Particularly challenging was the theory of evolution put forward by the English naturalist Charles Darwin (1809–1882), which seemed to imply that life itself might be the product of blind forces. Yet, precisely because it relied so much on rational explanations, the scientific worldview could not offer the spiritual consolation of traditional religions, which is why the challenge of science, far from destroying traditional religions, seems to have stimulated new forms of religious activity, such as evangelical forms of Christianity.

Outside the Atlantic core region the indirect effects of the Industrial Revolution were largely destructive as the growing political, commercial,

Thought Experiment

Public education for all is a very recent phenomenon in the scope of human history. Consider that public education in the nineteenth century reached many more people than ever before, but not as many as you might think. In 1900, only 51 percent of Americans age 5–19 were enrolled in school. Now imagine if there were no public schools or mandatory attendance. What would you be able to learn on your own? What wouldn't you be able to learn? For example, who would teach you to read if your parents weren't literate? Or where might you learn math? What kind of job could you have if you didn't even know basic math or could not read? Do you think public education is much more important in the modern world than it was in the agrarian world?

and military power of Europe and North America threatened traditional political and economic structures and eroded faith in ancient ways of thinking. Rapid population growth, land shortage, increased taxation, and new opportunities in the towns undermined village life in most of the world. As socialists pointed out, however, conditions in early industrial towns were often worse than those in the villages. Together, the slow erosion of peasant lifeways and the appalling conditions in early industrial towns created explosive social tensions in all industrializing societies.

Governments outside the core region of the early Industrial Revolution had to face the impossible challenge of trying to match European economic and military performance without undermining the traditional social and cultural structures on which their own power was based. The transition was bound to be painful because the dominant polities of the agrarian era had been based primarily on traditional forms of landlordship rather than on commerce; yet, people increasingly realized that industrialization was linked closely with commercial activity. Not surprisingly, the creation of modern forms of government frequently led to the violent breakdown of traditional social structures and systems of rule. Japan was one of the few traditional societies that managed to make a transition to a modern industrial economy without destroying the fabric of its society.

By 1900 many features of the modern revolution were apparent throughout the North Atlantic core region, and, for better or worse, many other parts of the world were also beginning to feel its impact on lifeways, economies, governments, and ways of thinking.

Twentieth-century Crisis: 1914–1945

Between 1913 and 1950 the engine of growth that had transformed so much of the world seemed to stall. Global rates of growth of GDP slowed from 1.30 percent per annum between 1870 and 1913 to 0.91 percent between 1913 and 1950. The slowdown affected all the core regions of the Industrial Revolution but was even more pronounced in the former agrarian colossi, China and India. The apparent exception to the rule was Russia, whose annual growth rate rose from 1.06 percent during the late czarist period, to 1.76 percent between 1913 and 1950, during the early Soviet period.

The slowdown was caused in part by a breakdown in the international banking and trading systems that had helped spread the Industrial Revolution. Between 1870 and 1950 the proportion of world production that was traded internationally actually fell. Part of the problem was that the governments of industrializing countries were still learning how best to manage rapid economic growth, and all too often, like the great agrarian empires of the past, they treated growth as a zero-sum game (a situation in which a gain for one side entails a loss for the other side) that could be won only by excluding rivals from protected markets. The burst of imperialism during the late nineteenth century was the most obvious expression of this rivalry as European nations tried to monopolize control of other parts of the world. Another expression of great power rivalry was the spread of protectionism (protection of domestic producers through restrictions on foreign competitors), and a third was the emergence of a system of defensive alliances in Europe, which helped turn a crisis in the Balkans into a global war. Distrust and rivalry among the major industrial powers clogged the arteries of international exchange that were so crucial to economic growth and political stability.

Topics for Further Study

Communism and Socialism

Fascism

Genocide

World War I

World War II

After the assassination of Archduke Francis Ferdinand, the heir to the throne of the Austro-Hungarian empire, on 28 June 1914, Austria invaded Serbia, Russia intervened to defend Serbia, and Germany declared war on Russia, which dragged Russia's allies, Britain and France, into the war. The global reach of European colonial and commercial networks pulled other regions into the war. German colonies in Africa, the Pacific, and China were seized by French, British, and Japanese armies; troops and supplies came to Europe from present and former colonies in India, southeastern Asia, Africa, Australasia, and North America as well as from semi-colonies such as Argentina. In 1917 the United States entered the war against Germany.

Nineteenth-century military innovations ensured that World War I would be particularly bloody. New weapons included machine guns, tanks, airplanes, and chemical weapons such as mustard gas, which could burn out the internal organs of its victims. Ironically, medical improvements kept more troops at the front, only to be slaughtered in the thousands by machine guns or artillery in often futile raids on enemy positions.

Extract from *All Quiet on the Western Front*

Since its publication in 1929, All Quiet on the Western Front *has remained a classic novel about the personal anguish of soldiers in war. German writer Erich Maria Remarque (1898–1970) based the novel on his own experiences as a soldier during World War I. Below is one of the most profound quotes from the book.*

But now, for the first time, I see you are a man like me. I thought of your hand-grenades, of your bayonet, of your rifle; now I see your wife and your face and our fellowship. Forgive me, comrade. We always see it too late. Why do they never tell us that you are poor devils like us, that your mothers are just as anxious as ours, and that we have the same fear of death, and the same dying and the same agony—Forgive me, comrade; how could you be my enemy?

Source: Remarque, E. M. (1929). *All Quiet on the Western Front* (A. W. Wheen, Trans., p. 223). New York. Fawcett Crest.

Modern industrial states mobilized for "total war" effectively as they took control of national economies to supply their armies. The home fronts—where women replaced men on the farms, in munitions factories, or on the railways—were as vital to success as the armies. Indeed, the vital role played by women during World War I was a major factor in the rapid spread of women's suffrage during the postwar years. World War I was not the first total war of the industrial era—the U.S. Civil War deserves that title more—but it demonstrated even more powerfully the appalling scale and destructiveness of industrialized warfare, and it was the first truly global war of the modern era.

Global Upheaval

A punitive peace treaty negotiated in Versailles, France, and the failure of the newly created League of Nations ensured that the rivalries that had caused World War I did not go away. In 1929 the international trading and banking system finally collapsed, leading to a depression that affected all the major capitalist powers, as well as the Asian, Latin American, and African countries that supplied them with raw materials. The Great Depression seemed to confirm the socialist prediction that the capitalist system would eventually break down. Many governments retreated even further into autarky (national economic self-sufficiency and independence) as they saw themselves competing for a dwindling share of world resources and markets.

In 1933 in Germany a fascist government emerged led by Adolf Hitler (1889–1945). Hitler was determined to reverse the losses of World War I, if necessary through conquest. Fascism also took hold in Italy, the birthplace of fascism's founder, Benito Mussolini (1883–1945), as well as in Spain, Brazil, and elsewhere. Fascism and socialism both reflected a deep disillusionment with the liberal capitalist ideologies of the late nineteenth century, but whereas fascists anticipated an era of national and racial conflict, in which the fittest and most powerful would triumph, revolutionary socialists framed the conflict in terms of class war that would pit capitalism against socialism, and capitalists against workers.

The appearance in Russia of a Marxist-inspired socialist state determined to overthrow capitalism was another apparent sign of the breakdown of nineteenth-century capitalism. Russia's czarist government had encouraged industrial growth but had failed (unlike the Meiji government

Worth Debating

In 1935 Sinclair Lewis's novel *It Can't Happen Here* was published. The plot dealt with how fascism could *indeed* happen here in the United States. Other fictional works, such as Philip Roth's 2004 novel, *The Plot Against America*, have posed similar scenarios. Do *you* think fascism could ever win out in America? What factors would have to be in place—or out of place—for that to occur?

in Japan) to incorporate within its ruling structures the entrepreneurs who would be needed to make a success of industrialization. Eventually the rapid growth of an urban proletariat (working class) and the impoverishment of increasing numbers of peasants generated a social crisis that, when combined with military defeat during the Russo-Japanese War and the huge costs of participation in World War I, led to the collapse of the Russian imperial state. Traditional elites reacted too passively to the crisis, which allowed the Bolsheviks, led by Vladimir Lenin (1870–1924), to seize power and hold on to it during a brutal civil war (1918–1920).

The Bolsheviks were radical Marxists, committed to the overthrow of world capitalism and its replacement by a society in which productive resources such as the land, banks, and all large enterprises would be owned collectively. Under Lenin's successor, Joseph Stalin (1879–1953), the Soviet government took decisive and brutal steps to build up a non-capitalist industrial society capable of challenging the might of its capitalist rivals. Employing methods of state management pioneered during World War I, the Soviet government began to manage and co-ordinate the entire Soviet economy, leaving no significant role to market forces. To manage rapid industrialization and rearmament, the Soviet government created a huge, powerful, and coercive state apparatus, willing and capable of acting with extreme brutality where necessary. For a time people thought the new system might match the economic and military power of the major capitalist states. During the 1930s and again during the 1950s rates of economic growth were more rapid in the Soviet Union than elsewhere (although the lack of market prices in the Soviet command economy makes monetary comparisons difficult). But, as became apparent later, the Soviet Union paid a terrible human cost for rapid industrialization.

REARMAMENT

During the 1930s, in an international climate of increasing tension, all the major powers began to re-arm. World War II began with attempts by Japan and Germany to create their own land empires. Japan invaded Manchuria in 1931 and China proper in 1937; Germany's expansionist drive led to war in Europe in 1939 after Germany invaded Poland. In 1941 the United States, now the largest economic power in the world, entered the war after Japan's preemptive attack on Pearl Harbor, and the Soviet Union entered the war after being invaded by Germany. World War II was fought in the Pacific and in eastern and southeastern Asia as much as in Europe, but eventually the economic and military power of the United States and the colossal mobilizational efforts of the Soviet Union helped turn the tide against the Axis powers (Germany, Japan, and Italy). World War II was even crueler than World War I. Sixty million people may have died—about 3 percent of the world's population at the time.

The war ended with the use of the most terrible weapon yet invented— the atomic bomb. The first atomic bombs were dropped on the Japanese cities of Hiroshima and Nagasaki in August 1945. (Colonel Paul Tibbets, Jr., the pilot of the B-29 bomber that dropped the atomic bomb, had named the plane *Enola Gay* after his mother. The bomb itself was nicknamed "Little Boy.") Most of the casualties of World War II were civilians as the

General Charles de Gaulle inspects troops in North Africa after the region was freed from German control by U.S. and British forces.

Thought Experiment

In 1945, President Harry Truman decided to use the atomic bomb to end World War II in the Pacific. Consider that ever since people have debated Truman's decision to use this most terrible weapon and that more and more countries have "joined" the nuclear club. Now imagine you could advise Truman, knowing what you know now. Would you suggest other options? Do you think it is significant that the United States remains the only country in the world to have used nuclear weapons in combat?

aerial bombing of cities became, for the first time, a recognized weapon of modern warfare. The extreme brutality of the war found its most potent symbol in the systematic murder by Hitler's Nazi Party of almost 6 million Jews in what has come to be known as the "Holocaust."

By the end of the war Europe no longer dominated the global economic system. The new superpowers were the United States and the Soviet Union. Each had its own allies and clients, and each represented a different path to modernity. The size and power of the Communist bloc were enhanced by the incorporation of much of eastern Europe and by the emergence in 1949 of a Communist-dominated China led by Mao Zedong (1893–1976). By 1950 almost one-third of the world's population lived under Communist governments. Throughout the period of the world wars, economic growth was more rapid outside of Europe, particularly in the United States, the Soviet Union, and Japan, but also in regions such as Latin America.

The emergence of powerful anti-colonial movements in southeastern Asia, India, Africa, and elsewhere marked the beginning of the end of European imperialism. In India the Indian National Congress, established in 1885, became a powerful supporter of independence, and in Mohandas Gandhi (1869–1948) it found an inspirational and creative leader whose nonviolent protests forced Britain to grant independence to the newly created states of India and Pakistan in 1947.

Despite the crises of the early twentieth century, socialist predictions of the death of capitalism were premature. Technological innovation was rapid throughout the period; the internal combustion engine entered mass production, aviation emerged (first as a weapon of war and then as a new form of commercial and personal transportation), and chemical substitutes for textiles and rubber were first produced. This was the era of sonar, of nuclear power, and of oil. It was also an era of fundamental scientific breakthroughs, particularly in physics.

Other developments helped ensure that the capitalist engine of growth would revive and that the frenetic pace of economic growth of the nineteenth century would be resumed. The managerial principles that would help revive growth first became apparent in the United States. Two developments were particularly important: mass production on assembly lines, pioneered by Henry Ford (1863–1947) in 1913, and mass consumerism, a phenomenon whose importance first became apparent during the 1920s as ordinary people began to gain access to modern goods such as cars, telephones, and radios.

BUYING INTO CONSUMERISM

Mass consumerism eventually provided a solution to the fundamental problem of under-consumption, which had haunted producers during the nineteenth century. As productivity rose, some producers found it increasingly difficult to market what they had produced. From at least the 1870s people had realized that capitalist economies are prone to periods of boom and bust as productivity outstrips market demand. The business cycles of capitalist economies were the modern equivalents of the agrarian era's Malthusian cycles of growth and decline, but, in a striking contrast, the business cycle was driven by over-production (or "under-consumption"), whereas Malthusian cycles had been driven largely by under-production (or "over-consumption"). During the early twentieth century people realized that stimulating demand might be a more promising way of ensuring long-term growth than seeking protected markets.

In order for demand to rise, however, governments and employers had to ensure that consumers had sufficient cash in their pockets to purchase goods and services. Instead of impoverishing their workers, they had to raise their living standards. During the depression of the 1930s economists such as John Maynard Keynes (1883–1946) argued that governments could help revive capitalist economies not by cutting wages further, but rather by boosting consumption through devices such as the provision of unemployment payments. However, governments were already experimenting with such devices. In the United States the "New Deal" of the 1930s pumped large amounts of money into the economy through government programs mostly designed to boost spending by creating employment through the building of new infrastructure such as roads and dams.

For capitalist governments mass consumption offered another advantage that undercut some of the anti-capitalist arguments of socialists. During the twentieth century people realized that populations with access to increasing material wealth were unlikely to turn into the sort of revolutionary proletariat that the German political philosopher Karl Marx had envisaged as the gravediggers of capitalism. Mass consumption was the capitalist system's most effective antidote to revolution.

CRISIS AND INNOVATION

In many fields the crisis period of 1914–1945 was also a period of cultural revolution. The theory of relativity advanced by Albert Einstein (1879–1955), and the theory of "quantum mechanics," developed by scientists such as Niels Bohr (1885–1962), Erwin Schrodinger (1887–1961), Werner Heisenberg (1901–1976), and Max Born (1882–1970), challenged earlier mechanistic models of the universe. The Austrian neurologist Sigmund Freud (1856–1939), by showing the importance of unconscious

Worth Debating

Many argue that American teenagers have taken mass consumption to new levels—undreamed of by economists who theorized about mass consumption. Marketers love to reach teens, who spend more than $100 billion a year. Teen spending certainly pumps up the U.S. economy. However, many social scientists and media critics counter that our kids are constantly being manipulated by the media (advertisers, television shows, and websites) to buy, buy, buy—setting the stage for overspending and debt in adulthood. What do you think? What evidence is there to support either side? Is one interpretation more plausible? Does it matter if we accept one over the other? Can we reasonably hold both views?

Key Events in Modern Media History

1870   More than 5,000 newspapers are published in the U.S.

1876   "Mr. Watson, come here. I want you." Bell invents the telephone.

1897   World's first cinema is built in Paris.

1900   Estimated 1,800 magazines are being published in the United States.

1900   Total newspaper circulation in U.S. passes 15 million daily.

1920   In England, Marconi creates the first short wave radio connection.

1928   Television sets are put in three U.S. homes, programming begins.

Source: University of Minnesota Media History Project. (2007). Retrieved May 22, 2007. From http://www.mediahistory.umn.edu/timeline

psychological drives, challenged faith in the role of reason in human affairs. New art forms, such as cinema, brought artistic realism into mass culture, but also challenged artists and writers to experiment with new, less realistic forms of expressionism, from the cubism of painters such as Pablo Picasso (1881–1973) to the dream language of *Finnegans Wake* by James Joyce (1882–1941).

The new technologies of mass culture, including radio, newspapers, and particularly the cinema, offered new ways of influencing the ideas, attitudes, and fantasies of people throughout the world, and governments as well as advertisers came to appreciate their power.

The Soviet government was particularly creative in using the mass media to spread its ideas. The new mass media also helped create a mass culture that could challenge the hegemony of traditional high culture. Outside of the industrial heartland, the revival of traditional religious and artistic traditions, such as those of Hinduism and Buddhism, began to play an important role in creating new national cultures that could challenge the cultural hegemony of the North Atlantic region.

Contemporary Period: 1945–Present

After World War II the capitalist engine roared to life again to generate the most rapid economic growth in world history. From 0.91 percent per annum between 1913 and 1950, global rates of growth of GDP rose to 2.93 percent between 1950 and 1973 before falling to the more modest but still impressive rate of 1.33 percent between 1973 and 1998.

The international economic order was revived and re-stabilized by expanding markets, by massive reconstruction aid from the United States during the Marshall Plan, and by the creation of global regulatory institutions such as the United Nations (in 1945) and the International Monetary Fund (in 1947). After falling between 1913 and 1950, the proportion of goods produced for international markets tripled between 1950 and 1995. A revival in international trade and the spread of mass consumerism, first in the United States and then in Europe and Japan, stimulated economic growth in all the leading capitalist countries. For the first time significant numbers of consumers in Europe and Japan began to buy private cars, televisions, and radios and even exotic foreign holidays, made possible by the reduced cost of air transportation. A new wave of innovations in electronics, many stimulated by wartime research programs, ushered in the electronic revolution of the 1980s and 1990s, and innovations in biology, including the discovery of the structure of deoxyribonucleic acid (DNA, the carrier of genetic information), spawned new techniques of genetic engineering whose implications are still unclear.

Capitalist governments became increasingly adept at sustaining growth by stimulating consumption and by seeking the right balance between intervention and "laissez-faire" (a doctrine opposing governmental interference in economic affairs). Slumps during the early 1970s and the late 1990s demonstrated that the business cycle has not been completely tamed. Nevertheless, many of the protectionist illusions of the late nineteenth century were shed as governments realized that in a world of rapid global growth, the wealth of individual nations (even the most powerful) usually depends more on global economic growth than on the possession of protected markets. A clearer understanding of the economic

Topics for Further Study

Climate Change

Cold War

Consumerism

Globalization

and political realities of modern capitalism explains the decision of U.S. governments to finance postwar reconstruction in Europe (through the Marshall Plan) and in Japan, even if that meant turning former enemies into commercial rivals.

Partly in this spirit, and partly under pressure from indigenous anti-colonial movements, European governments surrendered the empires they had conquered during the late nineteenth century. During the forty years after 1945 roughly a hundred nations achieved independence from their European overlords, and another batch of new nations emerged after the collapse of the Soviet Union in 1991. By 2007, the United Nations had 192 members.

Industrialization spread beyond the core regions of the late nineteenth century, partly with the active support of the major capitalist powers. Economic growth was particularly rapid until the late 1990s in eastern and southeastern Asia, in particular in South Korea, Taiwan, Malaysia, Thailand, Hong Kong, and Singapore, all of which were influenced by the Japanese model of growth.

Rockets and Rubles

Global economic growth occurred despite the partitioning of the world into two major power blocs. The capitalist and Communist powers challenged each other militarily, economically, and politically. For several decades these rivalries threatened to ignite a third world war, fought this time with nuclear weapons. However, the Cold War was also a contest for economic and political hegemony. Both sides agreed that during the modern era economic growth is the key to political and military success. Yet the two blocs offered rival paths to economic growth, and for perhaps three decades it was hard to know whether the command economies of the Communist world or the capitalist economies of the West would generate the most rapid growth.

After Stalin's death in 1953 Soviet living standards began to rise as his successors steered more investment toward consumer goods and housing. During the 1950s the Soviet Union enjoyed a string of successes that seemed to demonstrate the technological dynamism of its command economy. These successes included the creation of Soviet nuclear weapons and missiles, the launching of the first space satellite, *Sputnik*, in October 1957, and the launching of the first human, Yuri Gagarin (1934–1968), into orbit in 1961.

Then, during the 1970s, Soviet growth rates began to slow, and disillusionment set in as Soviet citizens realized that their living standards were well behind those in the major capitalist countries. Although the command economy could indeed innovate when massive resources were devoted to large prestige projects, without the constant pressure of competitive markets it could not generate the steady trickle of innovations that drove productivity growth in the capitalist world. By the 1980s it was clear that the Soviet economy was failing to incorporate the new electronic technologies that were revolutionizing capitalist economies and societies. Soviet generals understood that this fact was a military as well as a technological disaster for the Soviet Union.

The failures of the Soviet economy tell us much about the driving mechanisms of the modern revolution. Soviet planners understood from as early as the 1950s that the weaknesses of the command economy derived from the lack of competition and the absence of any effective equivalent of the profit motive. Even during the 1930s high rates of growth derived more from a massive, and highly coercive, mobilization of labor and resources than from real gains in efficiency. During the mid-1980s a new leader, Mikhail Gorbachev (b. 1931), admitted that the Soviet economy was grinding to a halt because it could no longer keep mobilizing new resources, as it had during the 1930s and 1940s. The Soviet system collapsed because its mobilizational strategy of growth, like that of traditional agrarian empires, although effective in military crises, stifled innovation. The failure of the Soviet command economy provides ironic support for Karl Marx's claim that capitalism is the motor of modernity.

CHINA ADAPTS

Communist China offers an apparent exception that proves the rule. During the 1950s the government of Mao Zedong tried to industrialize using the methods of Stalin. However, the economic and social disasters of the Great Leap Forward (1958–1961, a period in which the Chinese government tried to force the pace of industrialization by abolishing all private property) and the chaos of the Cultural Revolution (1966–1976, a period of internal chaos during which millions were accused of anti-communist activities and subjected to exile, banishment, or death), combined with the growing rift between China and the Soviet Union, encouraged the Chinese government to retreat from the Soviet ideal of total state control of the economy. After Mao's death in 1976 his successors cautiously reintroduced elements of a market economy, and as entrepreneurial activity spread in China, economic growth accelerated. Capitalism was never entirely destroyed in China (as it had been in the Soviet Union), which is why, despite the survival of its Communist government, its economy has shifted with some success toward a competitive market economy.

Throughout the world economic growth and the many changes that have come with growth transformed lifeways during this period. Mass education was introduced in most of the world; thus, a majority of people in most countries were introduced to the basics of literacy. More and more people lived in huge cities as improved medical, sanitary, and educational services and increasing opportunities for wage work lured people from the villages.

For the first time in human history cities became healthier places than villages, at least where they were supplied with the basic amenities of clean water, sanitation, medical services, transportation, and electricity. Improved medical care explains the astonishing fact that in just one generation (1955–1990), the average life span of human beings increased from about thirty-five years to fifty-five years.

Urbanization transformed gender relations as families adapted to an urban world in which women's salaries were as vital as those of men. Women have become increasingly visible in government, in education, in medicine, and in science. Yet, true gender equality, like economic equality, still seems a remote goal. Worldwide in 1990 about eighty women were in secondary education and sixty-five in tertiary education for every hundred men, and only about sixty women were in paid employment for every hundred men.

During the 1980s and 1990s new forms of electronic communications and transportation and the reintegration of the Soviet Union (and its successor states) and China into the capitalist world economy bound the world together more tightly than ever before. This new pulse of global integration has come to be known as "globalization." Globalization stimulated economic growth in most of the core industrial economies and many newly industrialized countries, although many of the world's poorer countries found the costs of competition too high and fell further behind, particularly in parts of Africa and Latin America. For better or worse, globalization also brought the world's many cultures into closer contact. As television

The popularity of Western consumer goods is evident in the signs for shops owned by British and U.S. companies adorning a building in downtown Seoul, South Korea.

and radio became more common even in Third World countries, the cultural norms and consumerist values of the most industrialized countries became commonplace throughout the world.

COCA-COLA CULTURE AND THE BACKLASH

The influence of the United States was particularly pervasive as consumer goods such as Coca-Cola and U.S. styles in clothing, music, sports, and entertainment became familiar throughout the world. Yet, Western influences have also generated a powerful, and sometimes violent, backlash as governments and citizens in other parts of the world have tried, with varying degrees of success, to defend traditional, and often deeply held, cultural and religious values. The emergence of new forms of radical anti-Westernism is merely one reflection of growing resistance to Western values.

Increasing global inequalities fueled resistance to Western values. In 1960 the wealthiest 20 percent of the world's population earned about thirty times as much as the poorest 20 percent; in 1991 the wealthiest 20 percent earned sixty-one times as much. The successes of the most highly industrialized countries threw a harsh spotlight on the poverty of less industrialized regions, highlighting inequalities in income and in access to

Worth Debating

In 1999, the Himalayan kingdom of Bhutan became the last nation in the world to introduce television to its people. Many in this remote Buddhist country feared what television would do to its culture and its citizens—especially since this would be the first mass exposure to Western culture. The country's prime minister felt that watching the news on the BBC and CNN would expose Bhutanese people to the working of democracy. But with forty-six channels added, they were exposed to a lot more than democracy in action. By 2002, Bhutan saw its first wave of crime, with drug offenses, thefts, and murders. Would Bhutan have been better off if that first satellite dish had never arrived? Is ignorance of the wider world sometimes bliss?

medical and educational resources, and to necessities such as clean water and air. Although industrialization spread to more and more countries during the twentieth century, in too many cases it was incomplete or narrowly based on the trade in specialist commodities such as coffee or oil, or managed by corrupt militaristic governments that skimmed off profits or spent them on armaments rather than reinvesting them in education, health and growth.

Although the wealth and the technologies now exist to provide all humanity with basic medical care, clean water, and adequate food, millions still die from famine or waterborne diseases in the least industrialized regions of the world, and lack of appropriate education and services has contributed to the rapid spread of AIDS, particularly in southern Africa, where in some countries almost one-quarter of the adult population had AIDS during the mid-1990s. Peasants have become increasingly marginalized as traditional rural lifeways have been undermined by overpopulation, the fragmentation of landholdings, and competition from cheap overseas imports.

In much of the world, "modernity" has meant the death of the peasantry, the class to which most humans had belonged throughout the agrarian era. The collapse of Communism has created Third World conditions in much of the former Communist world as well. For many people, even at the beginning of the twenty-first century, the modern revolution must still seem like a distant dream. Directly or indirectly, the deep economic, political, and cultural inequalities of the modern world will probably continue to fuel bloody guerrilla conflicts in which small groups with modern weapons attempt to resist the cultural, economic, and military power of the wealthiest capitalist states.

BURNING THE CANDLE

Whereas many people have seen the dire conditions in the world's poorest countries as a sign of those countries' backwardness, others have seen such conditions as a warning of future dangers for the world as a whole. During the second half of the twentieth century it became apparent to many that rapid population growth and increasing consumption were putting new pressures on the whole biosphere. In *Something New under the Sun*, John McNeill argued that, in the long perspective, the changing human relationship with the environment may turn out to be the most important of all the changes that occurred during the twentieth century.

Population growth accounts for much of the impact as cities have gobbled up farmland and forest land, as roads and highways have paved over more land, and as farmers in the developing world have cleared forest lands to eke out a living. During the late twentieth century, however, it became apparent that rates of population growth were slowing throughout the world as urbanization, increasing education, and improved services simultaneously reduced the pressure to have large families and raised their cost. At present, it seems likely that global populations will level out at 9 to 10 billion toward the end of the twenty-first century.

On the other hand, consumption levels are rising in much of the world. As industrialization spreads to China, India, Africa, and much of Latin America, and as more and more consumers begin to expect the material living standards currently enjoyed in Europe and North America, human pressure on the environment will increase even as population growth slows. Environmental strains take many forms. Habitats invaded by humans are no longer available to other species; thus, current rates of extinction may be as high as during the most rapid extinction episodes of the last 600 million years. Some resources are already being used at dangerously high levels; this is particularly true of fisheries and clean water.

The most dangerous of all these threats may be the impact on the atmosphere of burning large quantities of fossil fuels. Carbon dioxide is one of several greenhouse gases—gases that hold in the Sun's heat and therefore tend to raise the average temperature of the atmosphere. Deforestation may have increased global carbon dioxide levels during the agrarian era, but the burning of fossil fuels since the Industrial Revolution has greatly increased these levels, from approximately 280 parts per million in 1800 to approximately 350 in 2000, and levels could reach 550–660 parts per million by 2150. The exact consequences of this human manipulation of the atmosphere are not yet clear, but they are likely to cause significant and perhaps rapid changes in global climatic patterns—changes as great as those that occurred at the end of the last ice age. These changes will flood many coastal regions, create more unstable climates in much of the world, and destabilize the world economic system by undermining fertility in some regions while raising it in others. Some argue that humanity has entered a whole new epoch in its history due to our species' ability to reshape our world: the Anthropocene.

Humankind has become a global geological force in its own right, but the notion that we might have become the dominant force for change in the biosphere crystallized only in the last two decades of the twentieth century. Many scholars now argue that in the last two centuries we have in fact entered a new geological epoch, the "Anthropocene." What is the evidence for such a claim?

The geological time chart—a system for dating events in the Earth's history based on rock stratification—contains several different types of time periods. The largest are the *eons*, such as the Phanerozoic, the era of large organisms, which covers the last 540 million years. The next largest are the *eras*, such as the Cenozoic, the era of mammals, which covers the last 66 million years. Eras, in turn, can be divided into *periods*, such as the Quaternary, which covers the last two million years. And finally, periods are subdivided into *epochs*. The last and shortest of the epochs is the Holocene, which includes the 11,500 years since the end of the last ice age, a period of unusual climatic stability. In his book *The Holocene: An Environmental History*, the British geographer Neil Roberts provides a fine, readable history of the Holocene epoch that can help put the new idea of the Anthropocene into perspective. A number of scholars have begun to argue that the Holocene has ended, because in the last two centuries we have entered a new epoch, the Anthropocene, a turbulent period of exceptional

Thought Experiment

Can you imagine the future?

Imagine a future that you like. How different would the world be from today's world? How many people would there be? How would they live? How long would they live? Would there be a world government? Or many small, local governments?

Now imagine a future you don't like, and ask the same questions.

Finally, imagine what you think is the most likely future. It will probably be a mixture of good and bad. Don't get too worried about whether your answer is right or wrong. The important thing is to try to imagine these future worlds because you belong to a generation that will help create them.

and unpredictable change. The defining feature of the Anthropocene is the transformative role played by our own species, *Homo sapiens.* For most modern humans, increasing human control over the biosphere has meant a vast improvement in living standards; improved nutrition, housing, and health care; better communications; and faster transportation. But in the last fifty years it has also become apparent that these gains may have come at a considerable cost.

In its modern form, the idea of an Anthropocene epoch is generally attributed to the Dutch climatologist Paul Crutzen. According to one account, at a conference around the early 2000s he became increasingly frustrated by claims that we still were living in the Holocene epoch and finally could not resist saying, "We're no longer in the Holocene. We are in the Anthropocene."

Although it began recently on geological timescales, the Anthropocene is noteworthy even on the huge timescales of planetary history, because it marks the first time in the almost 4-billion-year history of life on Earth that a single species has played the leading role in shaping the biosphere. We are also changing things very very fast. There have been occasions when whole groups of organisms, such as the first bacteria capable of photosynthesis, have had a transformative impact on the biosphere (the first photosynthesizers began pumping oxygen into the atmosphere) or periods in which particular organisms had a significant impact on regional environments. But never before has a single species had the power to transform the entire biosphere on the time scale of just a few centuries. As the authors of a 2011 paper put it, "The term Anthropocene suggests: (i) that the Earth is now moving out of its current epoch, called the Holocene, and (ii) that human activity is largely responsible for this exit from the Holocene, that is, that humankind has become a global geological force in its own right."

The idea of the Anthropocene is not just of interest to geologists or paleontologists. It should also interest historians and anthropologists and big historians because of the central role it assigns to our own species, *Homo sapiens.* The idea offers a powerful lens through which to view human history and to consider what it is that makes our species so distinctive. Historians may also find the idea valuable because it suggests a new and more precise way of thinking about the epoch of human history generally described, with deliberate vagueness, as "modernity." But the idea of the Anthropocene should be of particular interest to the emerging global-change community, specialists from many different backgrounds who study our rapidly increasing impacts on the biosphere. Crutzen himself has described the idea as "a warning to the world."

The Upshot for Humanity

In 1969, by landing on the moon, human beings took the first, hesitant steps toward leaving their home planet. These steps brought into focus some of the major changes of the modern revolution, reminding humans that the increasing power and complexity of human societies were bought at a price and came with many dangers. Humans now have the power to destroy themselves and to do much damage to the planet. Our increased power clearly has brought responsibilities for which we are ill prepared, and the great complexity of the modern global community has created new forms of vulnerability and the fearsome prospect of a major collapse, similar to the collapses suffered in the past by many overambitious irrigation-based societies from Sumer to the Maya. On the other hand, the immense sophistication and scale of the knowledge available today hold out the promise of a managed transition to a more sustainable relationship with the biosphere.

What remains unclear, then, is whether the modern revolution will lead to the emergence of a new global system capable of relative ecological, economic, and political stability, or whether the accelerating change of the modern era is the prelude to a sudden, sharp collapse that will drive many parts of the world back to the productivity levels of the early agrarian era, if not even further. Perhaps the fundamental paradox of the modern revolution is that on the one hand human control over the biosphere has increased spectacularly; yet, on the other hand we have not yet shown that we can use that control in ways that are equitable and sustainable. Are we really in control of our astonishing creativity as a species? We must wait to see whether the astonishing collective achievements of our species will prove ephemeral or enduring.

Appendix A: Using *This Fleeting World* in the Classroom

World history is perhaps the most difficult course for history teachers and educators to organize, plan, and then teach. It is not easy to bring the whole world's history into focus while avoiding the "one darn culture [or thing] after another" trap that plagues so much history instruction. Of course, developing coherent history courses at any scale, whether regional, national, or local (e.g., courses in the history of Western civilization, the United States or, say, the city of Poughkeepsie), is a challenge. As former history teachers now working with prospective and practicing teachers, however, we think the teaching problems are more acute in world and big history. Most teachers seem to think this is because they must fit more "stuff" into a course on world history than they need to for a history course with a national or regional scope. Compared with when they are dealing with national or regional histories, teachers seem to lack an overarching picture of world historical change over time that might guide them in determining what, from among all that "stuff," they should include in their courses and to help them see how the history fits together.

Consider, for example, what happened at a workshop we recently conducted for over seventy-five world history teachers. We began by asking them to tell a five-minute story of the history of the United States. Everyone got right to work, quickly identifying familiar eras and events, and then explaining relationships between them. Most teachers quickly and easily constructed a familiar story that explained the growth and development of the United States: almost all their stories included Native Americans, European settlement and colonization, the war for independence and the Constitution, the Civil War and Reconstruction, expansion and industrialism, the World Wars, the Depression and New Deal, the Cold War, civil rights, and more recent events. When we then asked them to create a five-minute story of Western civilization, again the teachers got right to work. In this case too, they were able to craft a story of Western history quickly; their stories included similar turning points and events, with almost all including the River Valley civilizations, classical Mediterranean civilization, the Middle Ages, the Renaissance, the Reformation, the Enlightenment, nation-states, exploration, democratic revolutions, and industrialism. These history teachers, who ranged from relative novices to seasoned veterans, seemed to have readily available and useful "big pictures" of the history of the United States and the West that they employed to narrate change over time and to locate, within the big story, historical details visible only at smaller scales.

When we asked the group to create a five-minute story of world history, however, the reaction was different. Few got right down to the task. Some struggled over where to begin the story, others confessed a lack of knowledge in certain time periods or regions of the world, and still others told a Eurocentric story that they made world historical by mentioning China or India. Unlike when they were tackling U.S. history or Western civilization, the teachers did not use a large-scale story to frame their thinking of the world's history. Without a readily available big picture, these teachers reported feeling bogged down with details, unsure about what to include, what to leave out, and how things were connected to one another.

If world history courses are to be anything more than a cultural cavalcade or a factual data dump, then teachers must find useful ways to determine what to include in their courses and how to make coherent connections across historical events, cultures, and facts. In our careers as history teachers and teacher educators, and through our research on the teaching and learning of history, we have come to see how important comprehending the big picture is to meaningful and coherent instruction. Unfortunately, as others have pointed out, the places where teachers have typically gone for help—teacher training, state standards, textbooks, or curriculum projects—do not provide world history educators with the big picture they need to make curricular and instructional decisions.[1]

---

1 See for example, Robert B. Bain and Tamara L. Shreiner, "Issues and Options in Creating a National Assessment in World History," *The History Teacher* 38, no. 2 (2005): 241–72.; Lauren S. McArthur, "Thinking in World History Education: Using the Work of World Historians to Inform School Practices," paper delivered at World History Association Annual Conference, Long Beach, June, 2006. A notable curricular exception is *World History for Us All* curriculum project (http://worldhistoryforusall.sdsu.edu/dev/default.htm) directed by Ross Dunn.

That is why we are so enthusiastic about David Christian's interpretive essay *This Fleeting World*. In advancing a theory about the shape of "big" history, *This Fleeting World* offers teachers and world history educators a valuable tool—one that we have used successfully with teachers—for organizing and teaching coherent courses in the world's history.

This Fleeting World as a Teaching Tool

This Fleeting World presents a big-picture narrative of world and big history not found in any textbook, curriculum guide, or set of state or national standards. It offers history teachers and other educators at all levels a useful way to think about the design and structure of world history courses. By focusing on a large spatial scale, David Christian not only succeeds in telling a coherent story of the history of the universe (in less than one hundred pages), but also demonstrates ways teachers might manage critical challenges inherent in planning and teaching world history.

Many teachers, textbooks, and history courses stay at the nation-state or civilization level, rarely zooming out for a broader picture. They thus keep the instructional focus on national or civilizational politics and cultures—an approach that tends to reduce world history to a serial study of civilizations or nation-states, with little attention to interconnections except for an occasional comparison to emphasize political and cultural differences. *This Fleeting World,* however, takes a different stance. World history, Christian argues, goes beyond "telling the history of this nation or that community" to focus on "the interconnections between people and communities in all eras of human history." Its purpose, in Christian's words, should be to "explore...the histories of women and men across the entire world, the stories that all humans share because they are human." The focus is on the story of us all and on the crucial turning points in the human story—of major changes in the ways we humans produced and distributed food; organized ourselves in communities; defined and explored and populated our environment; experienced, responded to, and often created "worldwide" crises; and increased or decreased in numbers. In transcending the civilization or the nation as the unit of analysis, *This Fleeting World* presents this story in three big acts: the era of foraging, the agrarian era, and the modern era.

Like all good historians, Christian offers valuable historical detail and rich evidence to support his argument: this is no vague thematic history that ignores historical content. Christian uses details precisely as they should be used: to support and illuminate the narrative of human history in a way that makes it comprehensible. In focusing on this big story, however, Christian does not ignore other scales on which students should study the history of the world. Although his narrative centers on events so large that even civilizations—let alone nations, cultures, and individuals—are difficult to see, throughout the essay he uses regional, national, and local examples to explicate large-scale patterns.

In so doing, *This Fleeting World* also helps teachers tackle a second challenge in teaching world history, namely, helping students develop meaningful links between big history and stories occurring on smaller and more familiar historical scales. Put differently, world history teachers often struggle to help their students understand the relationships between macro- and micro-explanations of historical change. Sprinkled throughout *This Fleeting World's* big narrative are suggestions for close-up study or for considering relationships between structure and culture. Christian offers ideas for pursing historical questions at a different temporal-spatial scale, for making comparisons, or for paths one might follow to locate evidence that might even challenge his big story. Just as a photographer uses multiple lenses—close-up, wide-angle, and zoom—to tell pictorial stories, world history teachers and students need to observe the world's history through several different lenses to understand the whole most completely.[2]

Using This Fleeting World to Plan and Teach World History

When we used *This Fleeting World* with the seventy-five teachers mentioned above, they were enthusiastic about it, claiming the essays gave them a frame that could guide them as they crafted their history courses, exactly as they had for U.S. history and Western civilization. We found that the table of contents alone offered the teachers a needed but missing picture of global change and connections.

That is not to say everyone agreed with Christian's perspective. Some felt he gave short shrift to world religions as agents of change; others took

---

2 We are grateful to Craig Benjamin for suggesting this useful metaphor.

issue with the fact that in Christian's narrative, economic forces trumped cultural or intellectual forces. Still others expressed concern over the relative absence of individuals in the narrative. At the grand scale on which Christian's story unfolds, it is difficult to see the accomplishments and actions of individuals, and for some teachers, that raised important historiographical and pedagogical questions about human agency and cause and effect. These points of disagreement do not detract from the usefulness of the book, however; on the contrary, they make the book even more valuable because they encourage teachers to use or to seek historical evidence to challenge the case Christian makes.

How else might history teachers or history teacher educators use *This Fleeting World* as an instructional tool to enhance course designs, lesson planning, and teaching? The list that follows is just a small selection of ways we have begun to or plan to use this piece to improve world and big instruction.

For Planning Instructional Moves along Different Scales of Time and Space

Learning to recognize global patterns, over both time and space, and connect those patterns with inter-regional, regional, and local developments are among the most important and challenging habits of mind developed through the study of world history. In providing a large global narrative and offering suggestions for more fine-grained studies, *This Fleeting World* provides both a model and a framework for including within a history course layered and connected movement up and down geographic and temporal scales. Since designing instruction that enables students to move through nested scales of historical time and space is quite difficult, the support *This Fleeting World* offers teachers in meeting this challenge might be its greatest asset. Certainly that has been the opinion of the world history teachers with whom we work.

For example, consider how *This Fleeting World* treats the Industrial Revolution through a brief description of three waves of global industrial change. Starting with this global pattern, teachers might then ask themselves (and their students) to move down a level to see up close what industrialism looked like in Western Europe, Russia, or Japan. Zooming down even more, teachers could plan to have students look more closely at the effects of industrialization on particular colonies, such as India, or on gendered or class relationships within and across societies. Then, teachers could have students return to the big picture to reconsider it after having seen industrialism in and across regions.

FOR CREATING COURSE AND UNIT DESIGNS

Not only does *This Fleeting World* help teachers construct a vertical view of world history through the technique of nested temporal-spatial scales, the essay also helps teachers develop a linear view of big changes over time. Thus, teachers might use the chronological and topical divisions in *This Fleeting World* to frame periodization and topical schemes for their courses. Throughout each chapter, Christian makes strong arguments for significant turning points in human history that teachers might use as logical breaks in instructional time (e.g., units or ends of terms). Teachers might also look to *This Fleeting World* for important global topics, such as "The Earliest Cities" or "Creation of Global Networks," to frame instructional units or shape assessments. The descriptions Christian provides of early cities or global networks can help teachers think about the big and lasting ideas students could develop from investigating these topics and may spark ideas for the details a unit of study on early cities or global network might include.

FOR STIMULATING STUDENTS' THINKING

Many teachers will want to use *This Fleeting World* itself with their students, and we think that is a very good idea. Students also need big pictures of the history they study, and so teachers might use *This Fleeting World* with their students just as we have been using it with teachers—to build a large-scale picture of the human story. We can think of many good reasons why teachers might want to use this book in some form or another with students at the outset of a course, revisiting sections of it at the beginnings and ends of eras and units. Doing so should help students attach the details of what they learn to a larger frame, which in turn will help them remember historical details and make those details them meaningful.

We also think teachers might use sections of the book to provoke student thinking, stimulate investigations, and encourage critical thinking about the use of history. For example, the section entitled "Coca-Cola Culture and the Backlash" is a succinct discussion of the growing global influence and consequences of the diffusion of Western values and products that would make a wonderful topic for students to take up.

For Helping to Prepare Preservice Teachers

In the United States, world history is the fastest-growing subject in the social studies curriculum, if not the entire school curriculum. Yet, too few teachers have training in world history, even those certified to teach world history courses. For example, teachers in Michigan need only to have taken a two-course sequence in a region outside the United States or Europe to become certified to teach world history. While *This Fleeting World* is not a substitute for substantive course work in world history, it can help prepare preservice teachers by offering a global story and plenty of ideas about world-historical topics and resources. In courses we teach to prepare future history teachers, we intend to use this book in conjunction and comparison with popular textbooks and national and state standards in world history.

Conclusion

Obviously, we are excited about the possibilities *This Fleeting World* offers world history teachers, teacher educators, curriculum specialists, and students. We are confident that people will find additional productive ways to use this book to improve world history education and help students develop a deeper and more nuanced understanding of the history of humanity—a vital and essential goal for us all.

Bob Bain, University of Michigan,
and Lauren McArthur Harris,
Arizona State University

Bob Bain and Lauren McArthur Harris are former high
school world history teachers with over thirty-five years of
combined teaching experience. At the University of Michigan
and Arizona State University, respectively, they study world
history teaching and learning, as well as working with
prospective and practicing history teachers at all levels.

Appendix B: Periodization in World History

L ike all storytelling, history requires a structure, and periodization is one of the main devices that historians use to create structure. Yet, the past is seamless, fluid, and continuous. There are few natural breaks, so any attempt to divide the past into neat chronological chunks must be artificial. Periodization always does violence to the complex reality of the past, and even the most conscientious attempts at dividing up the past involve some distortion. Any scheme of periodization must compromise between the often contradictory demands of clarity, coherence, accuracy, and honesty.

The challenge of finding an appropriate scheme of periodization is particularly complex in world history, which tries to construct a coherent account of the past of all human societies. The challenges are even greater for *This Fleeting World,* which tries to describe the past at scales that will seem unfamiliar even to some world historians. Inevitably, it will sacrifice important details as it tries to sketch out the larger patterns. For example, it describes the evolution of agrarian civilizations as a whole rather than the distinct histories of particular civilizations. It takes a very different slice of the past, one that is neither better nor worse than more familiar slices, but simply different. And because it is different it can show some new things and can show some familiar things in a new light. Perhaps the most important object that we can see at these large scales is humanity. At this scale, and *only* at this scale, it is possible to get a sense of the historical trajectory of humans as a whole.

But to do so we have to think in new ways about the problem of periodization. The next section discusses the particular problems that periodization raises in world history, some traditional approaches to periodization, and the compromise solutions that have been adopted here in order to tell the story of humanity as a whole.

Problems of Periodization in World History

The problems we face are theoretical, organizational, ethical, and technical, and may be discussed as follows.

THEORETICAL PROBLEMS

Periodization poses theoretical problems because any chronological scheme highlights some aspects of the past and obscures others. Whereas a historian of gender might look for eras in which the relative status and power of women and men changed (the granting of suffrage to women, perhaps, or the emergence of patriarchal social relations in early agrarian societies), a historian of war might focus, instead, on changes in weaponry and tactics (such as the use of gunpowder or the appearance of the first organized armies), whereas a historian of religion might concentrate on the appearance of the first "universal" religions in the first millennium BCE. Different questions highlight different aspects of the past and generate different periodizations. In other words, to choose a periodization is to make some rather arbitrary judgments about what is and what is not most important in human history. By focusing on a small chunk of the past, historians can avoid some of these challenges, but in world history periodization requires judgments as to the most important changes across all societies on Earth. Is there sufficient consensus among historians as to what those changes are? At present, the answer is probably "No."

ORGANIZATIONAL PROBLEMS

Periodization also poses severe organizational problems. How can we find labels that do justice to many different regions and societies, each with its own distinctive historical trajectory? After all, at any given moment a million different things are happening. Which of them should the historian concentrate on? The problem is peculiarly acute in world history because whereas neighboring regions or states may evolve in closely related ways, societies separated by large distances may have little in common. Should we place them in the same period just because they existed at the same time? Or should we have separate periodizations for each region? In that case we risk losing any sense of the overall coherence of world history. The modern history profession emerged in Europe, and many well-established schemes of periodization were designed to make sense of European history.

This is true, for example, of the traditional division into ancient, medieval, and modern periods. But such labels make little sense outside of Europe, although they are so well-established that they sometimes get used nevertheless. Similarly, Chinese historians have long used dynastic labels to provide a framework for historical writing, but these, too, are labels that mean little elsewhere. What would it mean to talk of "Tang dynasty America," for example? Is it possible to find labels that make sense for Africa as well as for the whole of Eurasia, the Americas, and the Pacific? Here, too, there is little consensus among world historians about the best solution.

ETHICAL PROBLEMS

Periodization poses ethical problems because it can so easily imply value judgments. This is particularly true if our periodizations assume that some eras were more "evolved" or "progressive" than others. School texts on European history have commonly used labels such as the "Dark Ages," the "Middle Ages," the "Renaissance," the "Scientific Revolution," or the "Age of the Democratic Revolution." When used of entire historical periods, such labels are by no means neutral. They were generally used with the clear understanding that the Dark Ages were backward, that the Middle Ages were transitional, and that real progress toward modernity began with the Renaissance. Such schemes carry value judgments about different regions as well as different eras because they implicitly compare the differing levels of "progress" of different regions. Until recently it was commonly argued that while Western societies had modernized, many other societies had been stuck in earlier historical eras or stages and needed to catch up. Is it possible to construct a system of periodization that avoids imposing the values of one period or region onto another? For this problem, too, there are no generally accepted answers.

TECHNICAL PROBLEMS

By "technical problems" I mean the many problems that arise from the presence of numerous different calendars.

Why does it sound odd to say that "In 897 Columbus crossed the ocean blue"? Because to arrive at that date, I've used the Muslim rather than the Christian calendar. Ancient Greek city-states mostly dated events by the year of each ruler. Not until the fourth century BCE did Plato's friend, Timaeus, propose using a common system of chronology, based on the date of the first Olympiad. According to the modern (Christian) calendar, this was in the year 776 BCE. As these examples suggest, establishing a universal calendar has itself been a complex, prolonged, and difficult task. However, of all the problems I have described, this is the one on which there has emerged a reasonably broad consensus. But even here there remain arguments. Is use of the Christian calendar perhaps a subtle form of cultural imperialism? Can we escape that charge simply by using the abbreviations "BC/AD" (Before Christ and *Anno Domini*) or "BCE/CE" (Before the Christian Era and Contemporary Era)?

No system of periodization can solve all these problems or satisfy all these different demands. Like historical writing in general, schemes of periodization reflect the biases and judgments of the era and the people that produced them. They also reflect the questions being asked and the scale on which those questions are asked. This means that no single scheme will be appropriate for the many different scales on which historians can and do write about the past.

Schemes of Periodization

The simplest approach to periodization—one that is present in many creation stories—divides the past into two great eras. These can be thought of as the era of creation and the era of present time (as in some Australian Aboriginal accounts) or as the eras before and after "the fall" (as in the Genesis story within the Judeo-Christian-Islamic tradition). Dualistic periodizations offer a powerful way of contrasting the present and the past, either to praise or condemn the contemporary era. Traces of such periodizations survive, even today, in dichotomous schemes such as those of modernization theory, with its stark contrasting of so-called "modern" and "traditional" societies.

Most periodization schemes, however, divide the past into several major eras, each with subdivisions of its own. Dynastic histories weave their accounts of the past around the reign dates of major kings and emperors. Such accounts can be found in Chinese dynastic histories and in Mayan chronicles. Dynastic histories often imply a cyclical view of the past, in which each era (like each ruler) passes through periods of strength and weakness, or youth, maturity, and senility. Historical accounts conceived within a more linear view of the past often take as their framework a series of distinct eras, each of which may be seen as part of a larger, universal trajectory. Writing in the eighth century BCE, the Greek poet Hesiod described five great ages of history, beginning with a golden age, in which humans were contented and godlike, and passing through several stages of decline—the ages of silver, bronze, and heroes—and finally to the age of his own day, which Hesiod characterized as one of violence and stupidity.

Similar patterns of rise and fall have reappeared in more recent writings, such as in the work of Oswald Spengler (1880–1936) or Arnold Toynbee (1889–1975). Marxian historiography offered a combination of cyclical and linear chronologies, beginning with an era of simple perfection (the era of primitive communism), which was followed by stages characterized by increasing productivity and increasing inequality and exploitation. But the Marxist scheme culminated in a future that would resolve these contradictions by combining high productivity with a return to the egalitarianism of the first era.

Most modern periodization schemes have been linear. Such schemes have been greatly influenced by the work of archaeologists and anthropologists, for whom the problem of constructing a periodization covering the whole of human history was often more urgent than it was for historians. Because archaeologists, unlike historians, deal mainly with material artifacts, it was natural for them to construct their periodizations around aspects of material culture. And, at large scales, these seemed to point unequivocally to a history of linear change. The nineteenth-century Danish archaeologists Christian Thomsen (1788–1865) and Jens Worsaae (1821–1885) constructed a scheme comprising three ages—a Stone Age, a Bronze Age, and an Iron Age. That scheme still has some influence on the study of prehistory. In the twentieth century G. Gordon Childe (1892–1957) built on the Marxist insight that particular technologies imply distinctive lifeways and social structures to argue that the major turning points in human prehistory were technological and social. He stressed above all the appearance of agriculture (the "Neolithic Revolution") and the appearance of cities and states (the "Urban Revolution"). Nineteenth-century anthropologists such as Lewis Henry Morgan (1818–1881) and Edward Tylor (1832–1917) offered parallel schemes in which different eras were distinguished by different social structures in a progressive movement from "savagery" to 'barbarism" to "civilization."

In the late twentieth century historians, anthropologists, and archaeologists became increasingly sensitive to the dangers of using schemes that imply easy value judgments. So, although most modern schemes of periodization retain a sense of directionality in history, they usually resist the assumption that directionality implies either progress or decline. Then again, most modern schemes of periodization at the largest scales still rely primarily on a combination of technological and sociological factors to distinguish between different eras. This is a tradition with roots going back to the earliest written histories. The Sumerian epic of Gilgamesh, which dates from the third millennium BCE, recognizes, in the contrast between the urban warrior hero Gilgamesh and his great friend Enkidu, who came from the wild lands beyond the city, that different technologies imply different ways of living, different systems of ethics, and different types of political and social action. Karl Marx (1818–1883) formalized this insight within the notion of a "mode of production." The best justification for such an approach to the challenge of periodization is that fundamental technologies shape so many other aspects of human history, including living standards, demography, gender relations, political structures, ideas about the Universe, society, and the gods, and even the pace and nature of historical change.

A Periodization for World History as a Whole

The scheme that follows also hinges on technological and social changes. It offers a three-part periodization for human history as a whole, with subordinate periodizations within each of those major periods, which may vary from region to region. This nested structure is, inevitably, an imperfect compromise between various different goals, but it reflects a reasonably broad consensus within contemporary writings on world history.

Of the three major eras the first, "The Foraging Era," is by far the longest, lasting for more than 95 percent of the time that humans have lived on Earth, whereas the second, "The Agrarian Era," lasted for almost 10,000 years, and the last, "The Modern Era," is by far the shortest, having lasted so far for just 250 years. However, populations were small in the foraging era, so that, measured by the number of human lives lived, the agrarian and modern eras loom larger. Perhaps 12 percent of the roughly 100 billion humans who have ever lived were alive during the foraging era, whereas 68 percent lived during the agrarian era and 20 percent during the modern era. Increasing life expectancies in the modern era mean that, measured by human years lived, the modern era looms even larger, accounting for almost 30 percent of all human years lived, whereas the

❧ Three Major Eras of World History ❧

Major Eras (approximate dates*)	Subordinate Eras (approximate dates*)
Foraging 250,000–10,000 BP Societies mainly based on foraging lifeways	250,000–100,000 BP African origins
	100,000–10,000 BP Global migrations
Agrarian 8000 BCE–1750 CE (10,000–250 BP) Societies mainly based on agrarian lifeways 	8000–3000 BCE (10,000–5,000 BP) Agrarian communities before cities (later dates outside of Afro-Eurasia)
	3000–500 BCE Agrarian communities and the earliest cities and states (later dates outside of Afro-Eurasia)
	500 BCE–1000 CE Agriculture, cities, and empires (later dates outside of Afro-Eurasia)
	1000–1750 Agricultural societies on the eve of the modern revolution
Modern 1750–today Societies mainly based on modern industrial technologies	1750–1914 The Industrial Revolution
	1914–1945 Twentieth-century crisis
	1945–Today The contemporary era 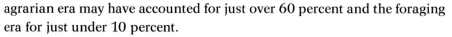

*before present (BP) and BCE/CE

agrarian era may have accounted for just over 60 percent and the foraging era for just under 10 percent.

As with all periodization schemes, we need to be aware of the limitations as well as the advantages of this particular periodization. The scheme adopted here takes as its basic framework three fundamental technological changes. These are the emergence of the first distinctively human societies, all of which relied on foraging for survival; the emergence of agriculture and of societies that depended mainly on agricultural production; and finally, the emergence of modern, industrial societies.

This scheme handles the organizational aspects of all periodization systems moderately well in its first and third eras. Before ten thousand years ago, it is reasonable to argue that all human societies relied on technologies that can be described, loosely, as forms of foraging, so that some useful generalizations can be made about all human societies. But it is also true that foraging societies survived in many parts of the world until modern times, so if we are to define this first era more precisely, we might say that it is the era in which *all* human societies depended on foraging for their survival. In the modern era, too, it is relatively easy to offer a global scheme of periodization because all parts of the world became interconnected, and all have been subject to some of the same forces and influences. So we can define the modern era as the era in which the profound technological changes of the last two or three centuries transformed societies throughout the world. The secondary periodization within this era reflects a loose (but by no means universal) consensus on some of the most important transitions within the modern era.

The organizational challenge is most intractable in the agrarian era, from about 10,000 BP (before the present) to about 250 BP. In this era, which provides the subject matter for most historical writing, the world was at its most diverse, and no single label can adequately capture that diversity. The histories of Afro-Eurasia, the Americas, and the Pacific world played out in completely separate arenas. Whereas in parts of Eurasia, agricultural societies emerged as early as ten thousand years ago, in the Americas all societies relied on foraging for several thousand years more, and in Australia agricultural societies did not exist until the modern era. The best way of defining this era, therefore, is to describe it as the era in which agriculture first began to have a significant impact on human societies in some parts of the world. But the huge differences in timing mean it is vital to opt for flexible subordinate periodizations within this large era. The scheme we have adopted implies the recognition of four broad phases in the history of agrarian societies. These phases occurred at different times in different regions. In the first there existed agricultural communities but no true cities and states. In the second there existed cities and early forms of states and empires. The third phase is distinguished by the emergence of larger and more interconnected systems of cities and states. The fourth phase is defined retrospectively by the understanding that, between 1000 and 1750, the world was on the verge of a transition more revolutionary than any that had occurred in any previous era of human history.

The best way of solving the ethical problems posed by any scheme of periodization is simply to take great care with language and labeling and to remember that all periodizations are somewhat arbitrary. The labels used here are intended to imply no judgments as to the superiority or inferiority of different types of society or different eras of human history. This periodization, however, clearly does imply a trajectory of some kind. On the largest scales there can be little doubt that there is a directionality to human history. Foraging, agrarian, and modern societies have not appeared in a chronologically random jumble but rather in a clear sequence. And that sequence has an underlying logic that reflects changing human relations with the environment. On large chronological scales human technologies have changed so as to yield increasing amounts of energy, food, and other resources, which allowed human populations to increase. This, in turn, has given rise to larger and more complex communities, whose technologies and sheer numbers have given them many advantages whenever they have come into contact with smaller communities with less productive technologies. There is a shape to human history, and that is precisely why a global periodization scheme of some kind is so necessary.

Further Reading

Bentley, J. H. (1996). Cross-cultural interaction and periodization in world history. *American Historical Review, 101*, 749–756.

Dunn, R. E. (Ed.). (2000). *The new world history: A teacher's companion.* Boston & New York: Bedford.

Green, W. A. (1992). Periodization in European and world history. *Journal of World History, 3*(1), 13–53.

Livi-Bacci, M. (1992). *A concise history of world population.* Oxford, UK: Blackwell.

Long, T. (2005). Periodization, conceptions of. In W. H. McNeill (Ed.), *Berkshire encyclopedia of world history* (Vol. 4, pp. 1458–1462). Great Barrington, MA: Berkshire Publishing Group.

Appendix C: Resources

This is a very selective list of resources in world history, focusing mainly on sources used in writing This Fleeting World. *The literature on world history is now very large and of increasingly high quality.*

Further Reading

Anderson, B. S., & Zinsser, J. P. (2000). *A history of their own: Women in Europe from prehistory to the present* (2nd ed.). New York: Oxford University Press.

Bairoch, P. (1988). *Cities and economic development: From the dawn of history to the present.* Chicago: University of Chicago Press.

Barber, E. W. (1994). *Women's work: The first 20,000 years: Women, cloth and society in early times.* New York: W. W. Norton.

Bayly, C. A. (2004). *The birth of the modern world 1780–1914.* Oxford, UK: Blackwell.

Bentley, J. H. (1993). *Old World encounters: Cross-cultural contacts and exchanges in pre-modern times.* New York: Oxford University Press

Bentley, J. H., & Ziegler, H. F. (1999). *Traditions and encounters: A global perspective on the past.* Boston: McGraw-Hill.

Brown, C. S. (2007). *Big history: From the Big Bang to the present.* New York: The New Press.

Bulliet, R., Crossley, P. K., Headrick, D. R., Hirsch, S. W., Johnson, L. L., & Northrup, D. (2001). *The Earth and its peoples: A global history* (2nd ed.). Boston: Houghton Mifflin.

Burenhult, G. (Ed.). (1993–1995). *The illustrated history of mankind* (Vols. 1–4). St. Lucia, Australia: University of Queensland Press.

Christian, D., Brown, C., & Benjamin, C. (2013). *Big history: Between nothing and everything.* Columbus, OH: McGraw Hill.

Christian, D. (2004). *Maps of time: An introduction to big history.* Berkeley and Los Angeles: University of California Press.

Cohen, M. (1977). *The food crisis in prehistory.* New Haven, CT: Yale University Press.

Cohen, M. (1989). *Health and the rise of civilization.* New Haven, CT: Yale University Press.

Davies, R. W., Harrison, M., & Wheatcroft, S. G. (Eds.). (1994). *The economic transformation of the Soviet Union, 1913–1945.* Cambridge, UK: Cambridge University Press.

Diamond, J. (1998). *Guns, germs, and steel: The fates of human societies.* London: Vintage.

Diamond, J. (2004). *Collapse: How societies choose to fail or succeed.* New York: Viking.

Ehret, C. (2002). *The civilizations of Africa: A history to 1800.* Charlottesville: University Press of Virginia.

Fagan, B. M. (2006). *People of the Earth: An introduction to world prehistory* (12th ed.). Upper Saddle River, NJ: Prentice Hall.

Fernandez-Armesto, F. (2007). *The world: A history.* Upper Saddle River, NJ: Pearson/Prentice Hall.

Flannery, T. (1995). *The future eaters: An ecological history of the Australasian lands and peoples.* Port Melbourne, Australia: Reed Books.

Flood, J. (1983). *Archaeology of the Dreamtime: The story of prehistoric Australia and her people.* Sydney, Australia: Collins.

Frank, A. G. (1998). *ReOrient: Global economy in the Asian age.* Berkeley and Los Angeles: University of California Press.

Headrick, D. R. (1990). Technological change. In B. L. Turner, W. C. Clark, R. W. Kates, J. F. Richards, J. T. Mathews, & W. B. Meyer. (Eds.), *The Earth as transformed by human action: Global and regional changes in the biosphere over the past 300 years* (pp. 55–67). Cambridge, UK: Cambridge University Press.

Heiser, C. B. (1990). *Seed to civilization: The story of food.* Cambridge, MA: Harvard University Press.

Hobsbawm, E. J. (1962). *The age of revolution, 1789–1848.* New York: New American Library.

Hobsbawm, E. J. (1977). *The age of capital.* London: Abacus.

Hobsbawm, E. J. (1987). *The age of empire.* London: Weidenfeld & Nicolson.

Hobsbawm, E. J. (1994). *The age of extremes.* London: Weidenfeld & Nicolson.

Johnson, A. W., & Earle, T. (2000). *The evolution of human societies* (2nd ed.). Stanford, CA: Stanford University Press.

Jones, R. (1969). Fire-stick farming. *Australian Natural History, 16*(7), 224–228.

Klein, R. G. (1999). *The human career: Human biological and cultural origins* (2nd ed.). Chicago: University of Chicago Press.

Kolbert, E. (2014). *The sixth extinction.* New York: Henry Holt.

Kolbert, E. (2006). *Field notes from a catastrophe: Man, nature, and climate change.* New York: Bloomsbury USA.

Ladurie, E. L. (1974). *The peasants of Languedoc* (J. Day, Trans.). Urbana: University of Illinois Press.

Livi-Bacci, M. (1992). *A concise history of world population*. Oxford, UK: Blackwell.

Maddison, A. (2001). *The world economy: A millennial perspective*. Paris: OECD.

Marks, R. B. (2002). *The origins of the modern world: A global and ecological narrative*. Oxford, UK: Rowman & Littlefield.

McBrearty, S., & Brooks, A. S. (2000). The revolution that wasn't: A new interpretation of the origin of modern human behavior. *Journal of Human Evolution, 39*(5), 453–563.

McNeill, J. R. (2000). *Something new under the sun: An environmental history of the twentieth-century world*. New York: W. W. Norton.

McNeill, J. R., & McNeill, W. H. (2003). *The human web: A bird's-eye view of world history*. New York: W. W. Norton.

McNeill, W. H. (1977). *Plagues and people*. Oxford, UK: Blackwell.

McNeill, W. H. (1982). *The pursuit of power: Technology, armed force and society since A.D. 1000*. Oxford, UK: Blackwell.

McNeill, W. H. (Senior Ed.), Bentley, J. H., Christian, D., Levinson, D., McNeill, J. R., Roupp, H., Zinsser, J. P. (Eds.). (2005). *Berkshire Encyclopedia of World History*. Great Barrington, MA: Berkshire Publishing Group.

Mears, J. (2001). Agricultural origins in global perspective. In M. Adas (Ed.), *Agricultural and pastoral societies in ancient and classical history* (pp. 36–70). Philadelphia: Temple University Press.

Palmer, R. (1959–1964). *The age of the democratic revolution: A political history of Europe and America, 1760–1800* (Vols. 1–2). Princeton, NJ: Princeton University Press.

Piperno, D. R., & Pearsall, D. M. (1998). *The origins of agriculture in the lowland neotropics*. London: Academic Press.

Pomeranz, K. (2000). *The great divergence: China, Europe, and the making of the modern world economy*. Princeton, NJ: Princeton University Press.

Pomeranz, K., & Topik, S. (1999). *The world trade created: Culture, society and the world economy, 1400 to the present*. Armonk, NY: M.E. Sharpe.

Population Reference Bureau. (n.d.). Human population: Fundamentals of growth, patterns of world urbanization. Retrieved August 27, 2004, from http://www.prb.org/Content/NavigationMenu/PRB/Educators/Human_Population/Urbanization2/Patterns_of_World_Urbanization1.htm

Richerson, P. T., & Boyd, R. (2004). *Not by genes alone: How culture transformed human evolution*. Chicago: University of Chicago Press.

Roberts, N. (1998). *The Holocene: An environmental history* (2nd ed.). Oxford, UK: Blackwell.

Sahlins, M. (1972). *Stone Age economics*. London: Tavistock.

Sherratt, A. (1981). Plough and pastoralism: Aspects of the secondary products revolution. In I. Hodder, G. Isaac, & N. Hammond (Eds.), *Patterns of the past* (pp. 261–305). Cambridge, UK: Cambridge University Press.

Sherratt, A. (1997). The secondary exploitation of animals in the Old World. *World Archaeology, 15*(1), 90–104.

Smith, B. D. (1995). *The emergence of agriculture.* New York: Scientific American Library.

Spier, F. (2011). *Big history and the future of humanity.* Hoboken, NJ: Wiley Blackwell.

Taagepera, R. (1978). Size and duration of empires: Growth-decline curves, 3000 to 600 BC. *Social Science Research, 7,* 180–196.

Taagepera, R. (1978). Size and duration of empires: Systematics of size. *Social Science Research, 7,* 108–127.

Taagepera, R. (1979). Size and duration of empires: Growth-decline curves, 600 BC to 600 AD. *Social Science Research, 3,* 115–138.

Taagepera, R. (1997). Expansion and contraction patterns of large polities: Context for Russia. *International Studies Quarterly, 41*(3), 475–504.

Weatherford, J. (2004). *Genghis Khan and the making of the modern world.* New York: Crown.

Wolf, E. R. (1982). *Europe and the people without history.* Berkeley and Los Angeles: University of California Press.

Wong, R. B. (1997). *China transformed: Historical change and the limits of European experience.* Ithaca, NY: Cornell University Press.

World development indicators. (2002). Washington, DC: World Bank.

Online Resources

Big History Project: https://www.bighistoryproject.com
Bridging World History: http://www.learner.org/channel/courses/worldhistory
Chronozoom: http://www.chronozoom.com/
Cosmos: A Spacetime Odyssey: http://www.cosmosontv.com/
The History Channel: http://www.history.com/shows/big-history
International Big History Association: http://ibhanet.org/
NASA: The Scale of the Universe 2: http://apod.nasa.gov/apod/ap120312.html
Welcome to the Anthropocene: http://www.anthropocene.info/en/home
World History Connected: http://worldhistoryconnected.press.uiuc.edu/
World History for Us All: http://worldhistoryforusall.sdsu.edu/dev/default.htm

About the Author

David Christian is a professor of world history at Macquarie University in Sydney, Australia, and co-founder, with Bill Gates, of the Big History Project. In 1989, Christian began teaching the first course on "big history," an interdisciplinary field that examines history starting with the Big Bang, and his work came to the attention of Bill Gates through a video course produced by The Teaching Company. He is the author of *Maps of Time: An Introduction to Big History*, which won the World History Association book prize (2004), and is writing a history of Central Asia. He is also the author of *Living Water: Vodka and Russian Society on the Eve of Emancipation* and (with R. E. F. Smith) *Bread and Salt: A Social and Economic History of Food and Drink in Russia*. He has spoken about big history at the TED Conference, the World Economic Forum, and on the Comedy Central program *The Colbert Report*.

Acknowledgments

The author would like to thank several world history colleagues for criticisms or suggestions about early drafts of this book. They include fellow editors on the *Berkshire Encyclopedia of World History:* William McNeill, Jerry Bentley, Karen Christensen, David Levinson, John McNeill, Heidi Roupp, and Judith Zinsser. He is particularly grateful to William McNeill, who for several decades has lent his immense authority as a scholar and writer to the task of writing about the past on very large scales. He also wants to thank Ross Dunn, Terry Burke, and the wonderful World History for Us All team for the intense, complex, and difficult—but profoundly interesting—discussions that came about from working on the WHFUA website. These discussions helped to clarify his own ideas on the overall shape of human history. His wife Chardi supported and blessed this project, as she has supported (and blessed) his entire career. He is also grateful to the staff of Berkshire Publishing for shepherding *This Fleeting World* through several printings.

Index

BERKSHIRE ENCYCLOPEDIA OF WORLD HISTORY 2ND EDITION

Editors: **William H. McNeill,** *University of Chicago,* **Jerry H. Bentley,** *University of Hawaii, Manoa,* **David Christian,** *Macquarie University,* **Ralph Croizier,** *University of Victoria,* **J. R. McNeill,** *Georgetown University*

AWARDS FOR THE 1ST EDITION	*Library Journal* Best Reference Source *Booklist* Editor's Choice *Choice* Outstanding Academic Title

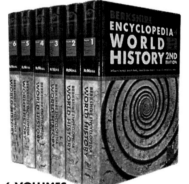

6 VOLUMES
978-1-933782-65-2
Price: US$1050
3,200 pages • 8½ x 11"

This landmark work has grown from 5 to 6 volumes and includes over 100 new articles on environmental history, world art, global communications, and information technology, as well as updates on recent events such as the Sichuan and Haiti earthquakes and the global economic crisis. Hundreds of new illustrations enhance visual appeal, while updated Further Reading sections guide readers toward continued study.

"A masterful title that weaves together social, scientific, anthropological, and geographical influences on world history, this set will be the benchmark against which future history encyclopedias are compared...[it] belongs on the shelves of all high-school, public, and academic libraries. In short: buy it. Now."
—*Booklist* starred review of the first edition

BERKSHIRE ENCYCLOPEDIA OF WORLD SPORT 3RD EDITION

3 VOLUMES
978-1-933782-62-1
Price: US$559
1,500 pages • 8½ x 11 inches

The renowned *Berkshire Encyclopedia of World Sport* provides comprehensive coverage of the culture, history, and business of sports around the world. The third edition brings the study of sports into the 21st century by integrating Berkshire's past work on women's sports and extreme sports into a complete sporting library.

The (London) Times called the first edition of the *Encyclopedia of World Sport* "the newest sporting bible." Berkshire sports titles have been praised by *GQ* magazine, *La Gazzetta dello Sport,* and the UK bookmakers William Hill, and received awards from *Choice, Library Journal,* and *Booklist.*

The 2013 edition is designed for use in world history, regional history, international relations, global studies, and other social science and humanities courses. It includes over 300 updated and new articles on sports management and marketing, branding, sponsorship, sporting goods, and technology, as well as on environmental and economic issues.

"This is an excellent and unusual collection of scholarly yet accessible material on the wide-ranging and rich world of sport."
—*Booklist*

BERKSHIRE ENCYCLOPEDIA OF CHINA

MODERN AND HISTORIC COVERAGE OF THE WORLD'S NEWEST AND OLDEST GLOBAL POWER

宝库山 中华全书：跨越历史和现代 审视最新和最古老的全球大国

China is changing our world, and Berkshire Publishing, known for its award-winning encyclopedias on a wide array of global issues including the award-winning 6-volume *Encyclopedia of Modern Asia*, is proud to publish the first major resource designed for students, teachers, businesspeople, government officials, and tourists seeking a greater understanding of China today.

"Take a publisher with a decade of experience in China, add a group of well-known Chinese and Western scholars, pay special attention to details (each of the 800 articles begins on its own page, all article titles are rendered in English, Chinese characters, and transliterations), add 1100 unique photographs, sprinkle in dozens of traditional Chinese proverbs, do it all on recycled, chlorine-free paper, throw in a year of free online access, and the end result is this sumptuous resource on all things China for the 21st century."

5 VOLUMES
978-0-9770159-4-8
Price: US$800
2,754 pages • 8½ × 11 inches

—*Library Journal* Best Reference 2009

BERKSHIRE DICTIONARY OF CHINESE BIOGRAPHY

宝库山 中华传记字典

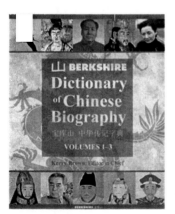

Editor-in-chief: **Kerry Brown,** *China Studies Centre at the University of Sydney*
Advisory Board: **Christopher Cullen,** *University of Cambridge,* **Julia Lovell,** *University of London,* **Guoxiang Peng,** *Tsinghua University,* **Chloe Starr,** *University of Oxford,* **Jan Stuart,** *British Museum,* **John Wills, Jr.,** *University of Southern California,* and **Frances Wood,** *British Library*

The *Berkshire Dictionary of Chinese Biography,* the first publication of its kind since 1898, is the work of more than one hundred internationally recognized experts from nearly a dozen countries. It has been designed to satisfy the growing thirst of students, researchers, professionals, and general readers for knowledge about China. It makes the entire span of Chinese history manageable by introducing the reader to emperors, politicians, poets, writers, artists, scientists, explorers, and philosophers who have shaped and transformed China over the course of five thousand years.

4 VOLUMES
978-1-614729-75-4
Price: US$779
1,840 pages

BERKSHIRE ENCYCLOPEDIA OF SUSTAINABILITY

10 VOLUMES
978-1-933782-01-0
Price: US$1,800
Discounts available
8½ × 11 inches

A ground-breaking interdisciplinary resource for 21st-century students and professionals, providing the knowledge and solutions we need to transform our common future. Over 1,200 expert contributors from many academic fields and from across the globe add to a comparative, cross-cultural approach, including different points of view and important debates.

"This is undoubtedly the most important and readable reference on sustainability of our time."
—Jim MacNeill, Secretary-General of the Brundtland Commission
and chief architect and lead author of *Our Common Future* (1984–1987)

This Is America

Edited by Duncan A. Campbell, David Levinson, and Michael A. Rockland

This Is America is a very short introduction to the United States of America, a nation that in recent history has been the most affluent, influential, and powerful on the planet, known for innovation as well as for its belief in its own "exceptionalism." In seven short chapters, the reader will learn the story of the nation usually referred to as "America," from its prehistory and early settlement through the twenty-first century.

978-1-61472-571-8 • Price: US$19.95 • 250 pages • 6 × 9½ inches

This Is Africa

Edited by Lorna Lueker-Zukas and David Levinson

This Is Africa provides a brief, engaging history of a great and too-little-known continent—a land rich in resources and troubled by conflict, now home to over a billion people speaking more than a thousand different languages. The book explores Africa's interrelatedness to other regions and cultures throughout history and examines its growing economic and political importance to other nations.

978-1-61472-570-1 • Price: US$19.95 • 150 pages • 6 × 9½ inches

This Good Earth

Edited by Brian Black, David Levinson, and Ian Spellerberg

This Good Earth: A Short History of Human Impact on the Natural World provides a concise guide to the often overwhelming world of climate change and related studies.

978-1-93378-286-7 • Price: US$19.95 • 150 pages • 6 × 9½ inches

SEND ORDERS TO:

BERKSHIRE PUBLISHING GROUP
122 Castle Street
Great Barrington, MA 01230-1506, U.S.A.
Tel +1 413 528 0206 • Fax +1 413 541 0076
cservice@berkshirepublishing.com
www.berkshirepublishing.com

PRAISE FOR BERKSHIRE'S "THIS WORLD OF OURS" SERIES

This Is America: A Short History of the United States is the latest in Berkshire's "This World Of Ours" series, acclaimed by some of the world's leading scholars. *This Fleeting World: A Short History of Humanity*, the first in the series, was praised by Bill Gates, founder of Microsoft and author of *The Road Ahead*. The books tackle big subjects such as China, America, Islam, sports, environmental history, and Africa—even the universe—in about a hundred pages. Each book is designed to be read in one or two sittings.

This Is China

"It is hard to imagine that such a short book can cover such a vast span of time and space. *This Is China: The First 5,000 Years* will help teachers, students, and general readers alike, as they seek for a preliminary guide to the contexts and complexities of Chinese culture."

> Jonathan Spence, professor of history,
> Yale University; author of
> *The Search for Modern China*

This Fleeting World

"I first became an avid student of David Christian by watching his course on DVD, and so I am very happy to see his enlightening presentation of the world's history captured in *This Fleeting World*. I hope it will introduce a wider audience to this gifted scientist and teacher."

> Bill Gates, founder of Microsoft

This Is Islam

"*This Is Islam* provides interested general readers and students with a concise but remarkably comprehensive introduction to Islam. It is a clearly presented guide that provides both a broad overview and important specifics in a way that is easy for both experts and non-specialists to use."

> John Voll, professor of Islamic history,
> Georgetown University

Forthcoming titles in the series include *This Good Earth: A Short History of Human Impact on the Natural World, This Sporting World,* and *This Is Africa.*

Notes